# SCIENCE
## *whispering*
# SPIRIT

BIZARRE PARANORMAL EVIDENCE

## Gary G. Preuss, Ph.D.

BALBOA.
PRESS
A DIVISION OF HAY HOUSE

Balboa Press books may be ordered through booksellers or by contacting:

Balboa Press
A Division of Hay House
1663 Liberty Drive
Bloomington, IN 47403
www.balboapress.com
1 (877) 407-4847

Because of the dynamic nature of the Internet, any web addresses or links contained in this book may have changed since publication and may no longer be valid. The views expressed in this work are solely those of the author and do not necessarily reflect the views of the publisher, and the publisher hereby disclaims any responsibility for them.

The author of this book does not dispense medical advice or prescribe the use of any technique as a form of treatment for physical, emotional, or medical problems without the advice of a physician, either directly or indirectly. The intent of the author is only to offer information of a general nature to help you in your quest for emotional and spiritual well-being. In the event you use any of the information in this book for yourself, which is your constitutional right, the author and the publisher assume no responsibility for your actions.

Any people depicted in stock imagery provided by Thinkstock are models, and such images are being used for illustrative purposes only. Certain stock imagery © Thinkstock.

Print information available on the last page.

ISBN: 978-1-5043-3980-3 (sc)
ISBN: 978-1-5043-3982-7 (hc)
ISBN: 978-1-5043-3981-0 (e)

Library of Congress Control Number: 2015914208

Balboa Press rev. date: 12/9/2015

To
MY MOM EMMA,
AND
MY DAD CHARLES,
AND
MY INTUITIVE FAMILY
CHARLES, JAN, DAVID, DAISY, AND HONEY

# CONTENTS

Preface: A Scientific Nerd Encounters Psychic Magic ........................ vii

## PART I
### Our Unlikely Universe

Chapter 1 The Magic of Our Universe ..................................... 1
Chapter 2 Did Anyone Hear a Big Bang? ................................. 8
Chapter 3 Einstein's Spooky Action at a Distance—
The Root of Psi? ..................................................... 12

## PART II
### The Reality of Psi

Chapter 4 Scientistic Reluctance ............................................ 20
Chapter 5 How We Got in This Rut: A Walk through
History of the Paranormal ................................... 29
Chapter 6 Can Psi Be Understood Scientifically? ................ 43
Chapter 7 The Best Evidence—Personal Validation ............ 52
Chapter 8 If it's Real, Why Don't Psychics win the Lottery? ......... 58
Chapter 9 Beyond the Statistics—How Does Psi Work? ....... 67
Chapter 10 Quantum Physics Hints at the Reality of Psi ........ 75

## PART III
### The Survival of Consciousness

Chapter 11 Whispers of Consciousness Survival ................... 84
Chapter 12 Consciousness...Now and after we Die ............... 90

Chapter 13 Our Brains Are Antennas—Not
              Generators—of Consciousness...................................105
Chapter 14 Living Outside the Body—Out of Body
              Experiences and Near-Death Experiences...................110
Chapter 15 Communicating with those Who Have Died ..............124
Chapter 16 Mediumship and a Whole New Language...................132
Chapter 17 Apparitions—Delivering a Message "In Person" .......140
Chapter 18 Keeping our Afterlife Telephones on the Hook..........146

PART IV

Reaping The Psychic Harvest

Chapter 19 Psychic Messages Coming Home ...............................150
Chapter 20 The Road Not Taken—An Act of Faith.........................159
Chapter 21 Harnessing our Miraculous Abilities ..........................168
Chapter 22 Conversations across the Chasm.................................179
Chapter 23 This Journey Has No Period .......................................189

Bibliography...............................................................................192
Index .......................................................................................202

# PREFACE

## A Scientific Nerd Encounters Psychic Magic

It first hit me when I signed up for an extracurricular course in college. I had noticed in an advertisement on a bulletin board that a Silva course, intriguingly referred to as Mind Control, could teach tricks for memorizing long lists. Being a bit of a left-brained nerd with a down-to-earth side that outweighed my esoteric bent, I felt the course was described as "mind control" so as to hook people to sign up. The course outline also hinted at improving one's psychic abilities, and although this may have been bait to make the course sound interesting, what attracted me most was a chance to improve my memory skills. How great it would be to zip through grocery shopping by memorizing a list of forty items. While taking the course, I indeed learned that, but I learned something much more valuable.

I discovered real evidence that the students in our course, including me, had demonstrable psychic abilities. This astounding evidence was based on doing "cases", which were experiments aimed at determining a stranger's health problems, a practice akin to medical intuition.

I was stunned. That is the best word to describe my reaction to the amazing results of my classmates and me. I knew we were not cheating, but somehow we were remarkably accurate at coming up with correct answers from what seemed to be imagination. Students were randomly assigned to pairs, and while one entered a relaxed meditative state, the second wrote down the name and condition of an acquaintance who had a notable physical characteristic, implant, illness, or handicap. Then the person meditating, presumably with brain waves in the slower alpha frequency state, was told the name of the person and asked to visualize his or her unusual condition. Although the meditating student could not see what the other had written on the cards, those cards served as documentation to verify if the meditating student identified the condition correctly. Toward the end of the course, our teacher had us again enter an alpha state and gave us verbal instructions to find his parents' home in Milwaukee, a place nearly a thousand miles away from any place I had traveled to in my life at the time. Decades later, I found the house, and the street was exactly as I had visualized it, with the curious error that the house was on the wrong side of the street. With an Internet search, I found that Silva teacher, now a professor at Washington State University, to verify the address of that house where his parents had lived three decades earlier.

In one case I particularly remember, I was asked to visualize, while in a meditative alpha state, the medical condition of a woman whose name I was given. On hearing her name, I immediately saw in my mind's eye what clearly looked like a bolt in her knee. I saw nothing else, as the metal bolt was so visually dominant. I remember feeling silly to mention that what looked like a bolt in her knee was the only thing I was "getting". The other person had written on the card that this woman had just experienced knee surgery and a metal implant had been put in her knee. If it had not been me, I would have suspected a "set up", but I had no clue other than a woman's name and a particularly adamant inner vision. Since it was my first case, I thought it was an incredibly lucky guess. But I got increasingly serious when such cases happened repeatedly while acting as both giver and receiver.

Yes, there were errors in doing those cases and some people clearly were better than others at those psychic games. But it also was obvious that the ratio of correct to incorrect "guesses" would absolutely have aced a statistical significance test. We joked about making up the stuff, but I was well aware that I had not cheated. We were paired with someone we did not know and had all made decisions on the spot about the name and condition we would present to our assigned partner. I knew I had not shared with my partner anything about the person on my list, and yet the number of hits was surreal, like living in the plot of a psychic movie. Nothing like this had ever been addressed in my education, and I was already in college. Since I was studying the statistical social sciences and had been interested in statistics since childhood, I knew these events were not all coincidence, given the huge number of possibilities that chance alone would have provided. I realized that the odds of repeated successes on highly specific cases were astronomically small, and yet here was real experience repeatedly beating those odds.

I was now confused about why something that seemed to work so well in the Silva course was met with so little interest or research in the academic arena. The professors in my social sciences classes were not providing any courses on these phenomena, and more bewilderingly, not even recognizing them as phenomena worth studying. The Silva course itself was not a university credit course, but was taught "on the other side of the hedges", which during my time at Rice University meant an extracurricular course taught off campus. My reaction was that something patently was missing in the dominant scientific paradigm about the ways of the universe. After personally experiencing multiple Silva cases and recognizing that there was a reality beyond chance, my confronting institutional bias against it was akin to reporting an encounter with a space alien and finding that no one with any authority was interested in uncovering what was going on. Although I had top notch professors within those hedges, psychic coincidences in the Silva class were simply not acknowledged as anything beyond entertaining fodder for a dubious publication like the *National Enquirer*. I was not belittled as weird for having had psychic experiences, but inexplicably, such experiences were simply ignored as coincidental.

This attitude gradually is changing. I know that Rice recently has fostered some excellent work in the wide-ranging paranormal and psychic field (which I will henceforth refer to as "psi", adopting the commonly used shorthand word to encapsulate psychic and paranormal phenomena), but the acceptance of psi in our culture has just begun. Cultural attitudes toward psychic and paranormal phenomena remain awkward and unresolved at best, so much so that a family relative recently told me that my earning a doctoral degree in parapsychic science was embarrassing, so I should not tell anyone.

## ■ The Road Ahead

· · · · · · · · · · · · · · · · · · · · · · · · · · · · · · · · · · · · · · · · · · · · · · · · · · · · · · · · · · · · · ·

My purpose is to share with you that science and spirituality are beginning to say the same things with different words. I want to share some of the abundant research that is finding solid links between science and the paranormal and spiritual. This will focus on three areas:

1. cosmology's evidence that our universe was not randomly formed but formed with a purpose,
2. the statistical evidence that psychic abilities are real,
3. the scientific evidence that human and animal consciousness survives physical death.

After this groundwork in the first three parts of this book, I will loosen up a bit in the last part, where I will share stories from a harvest of anecdotal spiritual guidance and other psychic anomalies in my life.

I believe that rationality is grounded in evidence, and the ever-so-gradual mounting of evidence now makes believing in what has long been called paranormal more rational than dismissing it as superstition. Science did not willingly move in this direction, but new discoveries over the past century have not fit neatly into the materialist scientific paradigm, so science is being nudged to broaden its perspective. Initially, I was inclined to limit this book to the scientific evidence for psi, particularly regarding the meta-analysis statistical studies done in Europe and the United States. But I found the evidence for the design of our universe and the survival of consciousness after physical death was tugging me to expand this into sort of trilogy of scientific evidence for paranormal and spiritual realities. The new physics is breaking down the institutional bias that avoided studying the paranormal and the likelihood of an intentionally designed universe, pushing science into areas long considered off-limits for research.

Quantum physics is one arena where science is finding surprises that border on spirituality. Its implications stretch what our perceptions have taught us, but we know that our perceptions can trick us. My quantum mechanics course at Rice was a totally technical course, with not a single clue that it hid any spiritual implications in its equations. The course focused on the mathematical probabilities of atomic electrons jumping from one energy level to another, giving us chalkboards full of daunting equations that seemed mostly irrelevant to anything except improving one's mathematical skills. It certainly looked completely irrelevant to the spiritual endeavors I was engaged in at the Catholic Student Center on the other side of the hedges.

Even today I remain rather stodgy about carrying this so far as to draw spiritual conclusions from scientific discoveries, as I believe that some New Age writers today are taking the spiritual implications of quantum physics too far. Some writers attribute spiritual dimensions to quantum physics that go well beyond the evidence of the physics, loosely tossing around the popular term "quantum" to include all sorts of imaginary possibilities without any confirmation or connection to reality. Nonetheless, science is finding itself forced today to accept more and more weirdness. For instance, quantum physics tells us that particles blink in and out of existence, and this on/off status has spiritual relevance, as does the role of observation in affecting what we previously believed was a physical reality. The implications are spiritual because they imply that something other than matter—perhaps consciousness or spirit—may be the fundamental units of reality. That the form of light changes between a particle and a wave depending on whether it is being observed is now genuine physics but it is far from the materialism of Newtonian physics. In fact, the Nobel Prize winner, Richard Feynman, noted that the double-slit experiment with light was a "phenomenon which is impossible, absolutely impossible, to explain in any classical way." (Gribbin, May 1, 1996, p. 164)

Light is fundamental to both science and spirituality, and the characteristic of light to exist outside of time is itself a bond linking science and spirituality. Light is the foundation of quantum physics, the physics that it forcing us to reject classical notions of a separation between science and spirit. Religious texts across the board, including the *Koran* and the *Bhagavad Gita*, portray God in terms of light, with darkness associated with fear and evil. In Christianity, God is repeatedly identified as light and Satan as the prince of darkness. The Gospel of John says up front (chapter 1, verses 1-5) that God is light and in Him there is no darkness. Christ is called "light from light" and the "light of the world" (John 8). It also appears that ordinary light has some type of awareness, which may sound scientifically ludicrous, but we know that the behavior of light in quantum physics shifts between a wave and a particle depending on whether it is being observed. Light is also one of the most fundamental cornerstones of near-death experiences, where experiencers commonly attempt to describe an intensely loving light that is essentially indescribable. The depth and nuance of this relationship is far from understood, and was the focus of an entire book, *God at the Speed of Light*, by T. Lee Baumann (Baumann, 2001). Perhaps the most intriguing link between science and spirit is evidenced by light.

In addition to quantum physics, myriad studies in cosmology have brought science to the doorstep of spirituality. Tenets accepted by religious traditions for centuries are finding scientific validation as well. Yet, the language of religion and science remain widely different in their perspective and descriptions. In referring to the beginning of our universe, for instance, religious traditions and science diverge widely on the particulars. But as we shall see, those particulars are not the interesting part of the story.

Religion and science indeed have different perspectives of reality. Dr. David Hawkins, in developing calibrations of consciousness, proposed that science cannot overlap with spirituality because they each exist in different realms. His consciousness calibrations showed that science calibrates at a level that stops at the doorstep of spirituality (Hawkins D., 1995). Rather like oil and water, the two are not enemies, but neither do they mix. The empirical methods of science provide us with predictability that has served us well in our physical world, but it is an ideology that may not apply to the spiritual dimension. Science studies electromagnetic energy and the weak and strong nuclear forces, but spirituality and psychic energy apparently are rooted in a form of energy not understood by science. In our current scientific understanding, applying a measuring scale to the concept of love is ridiculous, or at least incomplete, since love is so nuanced as to be indefinable in a scientific way. If it cannot be adequately defined, it cannot be readily measured, so the current tools of science fall short of the task.

Having mentioned these caveats, the situation is not hopeless. There have been scientific studies, for example, on the efficacy of prayer. Even with the difficulty of controlling who is prayed for, repeated scientific studies are coming down on the side that says that prayer works. This evidence for the power of prayer is statistical, which is to say that science does not pretend to understand why it works, but in as much as statistical significance can prove anything, prayer has a measurable effect on healing. This pattern is found with most research on the paranormal, with stronger connections when significant links are replicated. We have statistical evidence and spiritual acceptance that various paranormal phenomena are real, but there is a woeful paucity of scientific theory to understand what is going on.

## ■ Introducing Your Guide

I refer now to me, not spirit guides, which I will touch on later! I know you are not reading this book to know about me, but since a tour guide can color your experience with his or her biases, it is only fair that I apprise you up front of my take on reality. This is risky since we all see things somewhat differently, but I hope there is enough common ground for us to stay together for the journey. Human biases make it difficult to draw conclusions from evidence alone, but in my defense, I believe that my biases lie on both sides of the spectrum.

Although I find psi fascinating, I am mostly a practical person who feels a little uncomfortable in this woo-woo field. I am a rather unlikely candidate for writing about psi, as I grew up in a mostly rural family, and although my mother had some psychic experiences she would share, my bright parents were very down-to-earth. I worked for decades in a world of statistics and economics, putting emphasis on what I playfully call "numbers nerd" research. As such, I am my own worst enemy at second-guessing myself. Perhaps I worked as an economist for too many years, with the popular joke that having a one-handed economist would be preferable, so as to avoid the saying, "On the other hand...." Yes, much of me is skeptical about paranormal and metaphysical events, but there is another part of me that is spiritual and has experienced the paranormal quite personally, so I welcome any evidence that offers explanations.

The spiritual part of me is convinced that an intellect far great than ours exists and that we are a part of a grand design created by a loving intelligence. This part of me is quite pleased to see scientific evidence indicating that the universe's formation is purposeful, providing an impetus for writing this book. I may refer to this loving intelligence as God. I realize that the word God is loaded with interpretations, so my concept of God is not limited to a child's conception of an anthropomorphic being. For me, God could be a he, she, it, them, or none of the above, but remains an intelligence responsible for what we call the universe. It has been said that once you get your concept of God neatly tucked into your own box, you quickly get information that your box needs to be changed. It is the wrong size or perhaps it is the wrong box altogether. So I believe it is best to remain open-minded to all the changes that inevitably come in our lives, and I will attempt to steer clear of the term God because of its multiple connotations. Still, I suspect we share enough common ground to understand what I mean.

Yes, I believe in a loving, super, and interactive intelligence, but on the other hand, I am a skeptical numbers nerd who is uncomfortable accepting things on faith alone. I rather like the state nickname for Missouri, as I tend to doubt whatever you cannot "show me". Simply, my beliefs need evidence before I totally accept them. I have encountered a similar attitude among many of my friends, and if you are the same, this book may be just what you want. More and more scientific evidence is mounting to back up faith, even from scientific sources that have no intention of doing so. Unfortunately, evidence and proof are different concepts, but evidence at least points in the direction of proof.

Fundamental truths in religion can be recognized by flashes of inspiration, and the word inspiration itself captures the state of being "in spirit". But it is not difficult to see that religions have been contaminated by human error. Although suspicious religious teachings are probably grounded in a desire for good and are not professed with an intent to mislead, I am well aware of power struggles and human imperfections that cause us—religious teachers included—to miss the target. Consequently, I believe that religions are inclined to overstate what we know, harnessing faith or authority to make pronouncements that are grounded in educated guesses at best and self-serving disingenuous political motives at worst. The tendency of religions to say more than we know leaves us in a realm of speculation that actually may undermine faith. Even though I was a novice in the Society of Jesus (Jesuits) and maintain an active faith life, I am like many of us that feel uncomfortable with a church's tendency to make dogmatic statements that seem more grounded in social convention, tradition, or political expediency than in anything that we really know or that has been clearly revealed.

I seek the evidence of science but certainly recognize that it also has limitations. I once had more faith in the scientific method than I do now, but perhaps the wisest bit of insight I gathered during a stint of graduate study at the University of Chicago was from a fellow student. Because I had an inordinate trust in empirical evidence and tended to belittle any social science theory that lacked statistics to back it up, I disparagingly referred to such theories as "armchair philosophy". In fact, my initial interest in studying social science at the University of Chicago was that this program had a long-standing reputation for positivism, which was studying the social sciences with statistical rigor. While I was convinced that this was the way to go, this student pointed out that empiricism and positivism are "ideologies like everything else" (Raaberg, 1976). He was pointing out that my faith in the experimental method was placing trust in an ideology that was itself a theory. There remains a danger in putting too much reliance on statistical science, especially given that what we can perceive and measure through our senses is not reality anyway. Our senses cannot adequately capture what really is "out there". We create a reality in our minds based on the processed information we receive from our five or more senses, so true reality is something different from what we perceive. My eyes do not see reality but collect information for my brain to process and create its own reality. Because our perceptions cannot capture true reality, our science and personal experience cannot capture reality, and faith traditions influenced by human imperfections also are imperfect at capturing reality.

But given these limitations, the study of the paranormal is not hopeless. This book is an honest attempt to say yes when I mean yes and to say no when I mean no. The emphasis will be on verifiable evidence. I recall uneasy feelings that what I was told in church and what I was told in school often seemed contradictory. Humility was taught as a virtue in the church and often as a weakness in school, giving inconsistent and confusing perspectives for a child. Cooperation was heralded as spiritual nobility in the church, while school teaching tended to glorify the value of competition. How the world was created and humankind came to be was, or course, not a topic anyone could prove, but I was unhappy that the descriptions of reality varied by the source.

Having evidence is a step ahead of pure speculation. Years of scientific evidence allow global positioning systems (GPS) to navigate around our planet, using both the development and placement of satellites and their signals that account for both the speed of light and slight variations arising from the time and space adjustments of special relativity. This is one example of how evidence gives us a foundation that distinguishes what we believe from superstition, so what is being revealed in the realm of science and cosmology is more than what we knew before.

So I offer this book as an attempt to wrap up evidence that draws from science, personal experience, reading, research, and yes, the tricky area of personal revelation from my own spirit guides. If you are saying, "Whoa, what is this talk of spirit guides?", or if you do simply do not see what spiritual guidance and evidence have in common, I again hope you stay with me. Spiritual revelations give highly unlikely information that often can be verified practically in the real world. I have a desire for solid evidence, but I also rely on a Jesuit teaching about spiritual guidance; if one asks to be guided and refuses to be attached to a predisposed outcome, the answers received can be trusted. The trick is being aware and disciplined enough to test what may be erroneous. Toward the end of this book, I will share some revelations I have received and verified in this way. I hope to show that a numbers nerd can provide you with entertaining and useful discoveries.

## ▪ Bits of Anecdotal Evidence

You already know that I am convinced that psychic phenomena are real based on my own personal evidence. Yes, anecdotal evidence is shaky evidence, but enough such experience can convince us on a personal level that something weird, yet real, is happening. In a personal vein, here is a story that lent verisimilitude to any doubts I held about the reality of psi. Such personal experiences underlie my belief that we need more research on the benefits of paranormal and psychic events.

When I was in graduate school, my brother telephoned me at my research job at the United Way of America in Alexandria, Virginia. He said that he had a medical school interview in New York City on a Thursday. Considering that he would be flying from Texas, he said he would like to visit with me in the D.C. area on that weekend.

Even though I had to work on Friday, I offered to drive the 400 mile roundtrip to New York City to pick him up. So we were driving on the Kennedy Turnpike deep into a Thursday/Friday night, a highly unusual circumstance for a late night during the work week. At the time, my brother lived over a hundred miles away from my mother, who had not been told of his trip to visit me. She telephoned me at work early on that Friday morning. A call from her at my workplace early in the morning was indeed rare, but her reason for calling startled me. She had dreamt that Charles and I were in a car on a freeway, and her dream had been so vivid that she felt compelled to ask if her dream had meaning to me. The odds were tiny that my brother and I—living across the country from each other—would be commuting together anywhere late on a weekday work night. But yes, we had been on a freeway that night. For all my mother knew, each of us should have been asleep in our homes a couple of thousand miles apart at the time. I asked my brother if he had told our mother about this trip, and he had not even told her that he was flying to New York City for an interview.

This was not the only anecdotal event of a paranormal experience involving my mother. On a perfectly normal summer day in 1989, she had also witnessed the sun spinning in multiple colors. In this case, she was at our home near the Texas Gulf Coast town of El Campo, but miraculous healings had been reported hundreds of miles away at the St. John Neumann church in the Texas panhandle city of Lubbock. The spontaneous healings at that parish were getting much word-of-mouth publicity, so some people from El Campo had made the cross-Texas trek to the Lubbock church for a healing miracle that had been promised on that day. Although Catholic herself, Mom was deeply suspicious of miracles scheduled for a particular date. When the date arrived, she was outside hanging clothes on a cloudless and hot August day, thinking in her words "that all those crazy people are going to Lubbock in this heat, and they will come back sicker than when they went". (Preuss, 1989) At that moment, she noticed something very unusual out the corner of her eye. She looked toward it—directly at the sun—and the sun was spinning with colors of blue, red, and green. In her description, it was "spitting" beautiful colors away from it. She was entranced and stared at this easy-to-look-at sun in absolute amazement for "a couple of minutes" and suddenly remembered that she was babysitting my niece. She went into the house to check on the child, and on returning outside, she could not even look at the sun, which had returned to its blindingly bright afternoon brilliance. According to news reports, many people throughout the southwestern U.S. had witnessed this solar event that day, even though most people who had been outside at the time had not (Foundation, 2011). Before the news reports, my Mom was reluctant to share her experience for fear of ridicule, but especially after hearing about others that had witnessed the same thing at the time in many places, she told us. She was perpetually amazed by this magical experience and mentioned it often.

These anecdotal stories are useful for setting the paranormal stage. Decades ago, my aunt had gall bladder surgery that had some complications. While on the operating table, she had a near-death experience (NDE) where she met her deceased brother and father. In what has become a commonly reported characteristic of NDEs, they eventually told her to return to her body, as "it was not yet her time". Although this experience was hyperreal to her, this was before NDEs were studied and made public by researchers such as Raymond Moody, so my mother may have been the only person with whom my aunt initially shared this experience. My mother eventually told our family about this, providing yet another intriguing experience of the paranormal. Such NDEs and other paranormal events are the fodder that presented an impetus for this book.

We may not get a scientific explanation, but there is no harm in harnessing science to study such phenomena and reporting what it finds. And despite the remaining professional pressures, I am thankful that there is now research that offers its own statistical evidence, most notably from the Institute of Noetic Sciences, but also from Duke, Princeton (PEAR), the Windbridge Institute, the International Society for the Study of Subtle Energy and Energy Medicine (ISSSEEM), the International Association for Near Death Studies (IANDS), and various British universities. That is the fun on the agenda, so to begin, let's look at some quirky but incredible scientific oddities that cosmology has unwrapped about our universe's almost absurdly unlikely probability to exist as it does.

# PART I

## OUR UNLIKELY UNIVERSE

# CHAPTER

## 1

# THE MAGIC OF OUR UNIVERSE

> There may be no such thing as...a central mechanism of
> the universe. Not machinery but magic may be a better
> description of the treasure that is waiting.
>
> --Quantum Physicist John Wheeler
> (Herbert, 1985, p. 29)

SCIENCE IS REVEALING A UNIVERSE that is indeed magical, and the magic is
eerily similar to what religious traditions have long embraced. Yes,
it is grounded in serious experimentation, but what is discovered
seems unreal to our senses, so I prefer to call it magical. It is magical
enough that the universe even exists, based on what we know about
gravity, atomic forces, and probability, as the likelihood of it coming
into being is absolutely miniscule unless it was somehow intended. I
realize that this may sound presumptuous, but this blanket statement
has solid evidence behind it. Science has uncovered enough
peculiarities about the universe to realize that the probability of our
universe arising by chance is almost statistically impossible.

One of the more enthralling facts uncovered early in the twentieth
century is that our universe is expanding. This fact hardly shakes one's
boat and may sound rather irrelevant and unenchanting in itself, but
its implications are quite revelatory. Expansion was theorized by the

Dutch astronomer Willem de Sitter, but like so many pioneering theories of astronomy, his theory was initially ridiculed. Obviously, no one felt any motion on our planet, and the universe was assumed to be static, endlessly repeating its same cycles of motion in the same place. Albert Einstein first rejected the notion of an expanding universe, but the red shifting of light from stars revealed that *all* the stars were moving away from us. Einstein struggled to accept expansion, a theory which created a mathematical nightmare, and in a classic case of new scientific evidence that forced a review of accepted concepts, he actually remarked that it irritated him. Vesto Slipher, Milton Humason, and Edwin Hubble developed Hubble's Law and eventually provided the astronomical proof that the universe is expanding in all directions.

The sensational part lies in the rate of expansion. If this rate was increased by a tiny amount—"just a trillionth of a trillionth of a trillionth of one percent", as described by the mathematical cosmologist Brian Swimme in *Canticle of the Cosmos,* atomic forces would be too weak to allow matter ever to become more than simple atoms (Swimme, 1990). Given what physics has ascertained about the binding forces of atoms, no molecular combinations could remain steady with the weaker binding forces of (an ever-so-slightly) faster expansion, so no heavy elements would be stable enough to form. "No heavy elements" means no planets, no animal life, and yes, no anything except boring atoms. The verification of the rate of expansion meant that there was an obvious upper limit on the speed of expansion, and our universe was awfully close to this limit. How lucky we were that it was not just a tad faster. On the other side, how much slower could the rate of expansion have been before it encountered some other cataclysmic consequence? It turns out to be not much. Not even a little bit, in fact. "If you decreased the expansion rate by a trillionth of a trillionth of a trillionth of one percent, the universe would expand for a few million years, hatch a few atoms, and then collapse. That would be it." (Swimme, 1990) That is, the expansion rate would not be great enough to counteract the gravity of all the stars and other matter, and the universe eventually would crunch in on itself.

So, if you are not amazed by this tiny window of opportunity that allows our universe to exist at all, brush up a bit on your statistics. A trillionth of a trillionth of a trillionth of one percent on one side or the other leaves almost nothing to chance. Science has revealed that for our universe to emerge as it is, with its vibrant creation of stars and yes, life, the slit of possibilities is so infinitesimally small that its existence is asymptotically close to impossible. An example can elucidate how unlikely this is statistically. It is akin to the probability of shooting a bullet from the earth to a target on the surface of the moon—having only one shot to do so—and needing to be so accurate that the bullet would require grease to slide cleanly through a narrow target cylinder on the moon. The odds for our universe to exist in a way that can support life make the odds of winning a lottery jackpot look insipidly routine!

But if that is not enough to float your duck, I want to share the description of such a tiny probability shared by the popular author Wayne Dyer, used as evidence for faith in his book, *There's a Spiritual Solution to Every Problem*. For all his wealth of talent, Wayne Dyer is no statistician, but he shared an excellent illustrative example originally published by John Horgan (Horgan, November 25, 1996) that describes what a "trillionth of a trillionth of a trillionth of one percent" probability would look like. He describes a tornado that roars through a junk yard, and the tornadic winds whip everything around. As the tornado moves on, it has rammed the junk together into a mass that looks exactly like a 747 jetliner, complete with engine, seats, fuel tanks, and instruments. When fueled, this cobbled junk works like a 747 jetliner. This seemingly impossible scenario is possible at a tiny likelihood of about a trillionth of a trillionth of a trillionth of one percent. Such is the probability our universe had of coming into existence and remaining so, based on scientific information on atomic forces, gravity, and the witnessed rate of expansion. Our universe is a living model of that working 747 thrown together by a tornado.

What this indicates is an *intention* to produce stars and life. This tiny probability that our universe exists is not proof of intention, but it is overwhelmingly powerful evidence that the characteristics of our universe did not arise by chance. Exploring this a bit, philosophy's anthropic principle allows that as long as something is not impossible, it can arise by chance. It allows that one way for this to be possible would be an infinity of dead universes, where we just happen to be part of an infinitesimally unlikely one. The fact that we can observe our universe at all is because we are conscious, and if we were in almost any of the other universes, we would not exist in any conscious way. There may be a gazillion universes where consciousness does not exist, and we are obviously in an unusual universe to have the capacity to witness it. All those other universes are the normal ones, basically full of randomness and disorder. Because of our consciousness, ours is exceptionally weird.

But there is another reason our universe should not exist in the form it does. According to the second law of thermodynamics, a universe so highly ordered as to allow consciousness to exist violates the laws of entropy, unless something is manipulating it. This law says that everything is ruled by entropy, which says that if left unchecked, order will always give way to disorder. Entropy is very obvious to anyone living in our physical world. If you build a house and never do anything with it, climate and time will reduce it to rubble in a few centuries and to dust in a few millennia. Entropy would take a house back to the raw materials that comprise it, which are more disordered than the construction materials. In fact, because of entropy, no house will take shape from raw materials unless a builder intervenes to manipulate those materials. So it would go with our universe without design and maintenance, but that is not what we see. Our universe clearly is more than random matter and space, and the existence and birth of new suns and planets, not to mention life and consciousness, are highly ordered states. Without a builder, our universe effectively violates the second law of thermodynamics.

A philosophical way around this limitation, which would allow our universe to exist as it is without an external force of maintenance, again would be to have an infinite number of universes, but this obviously has its own scientific doorstop. With an infinite number of universes, everything can and will happen, regardless of how unlikely it is. For example, with an infinite number of rooms filled with oxygen, there are ordinary rooms where you would die from asphyxiation. That is, all the oxygen atoms, based on a probability distribution alone, would collect in a different part of the room, leaving none in every place in the room where you were trying to breathe. The probability of gazillions of oxygen atoms randomly distributing themselves this way without an external force, like the probability of our universe existing as it does, is so remote as to be nearly impossible. But it would still happen in the case where an infinite number of rooms exist. Although allowing a way for this to happen, the concept of an infinite number of universes violates another commonly held scientific theory—Occam's razor—which says that the most plausible explanation for something happening is the simplest explanation—the one requiring the fewest number of assumptions.

Physical life itself violates the concept of entropy, since without an underlying designer, entropy would not allow cosmic material to reach a thermodynamic equilibrium sufficient for life to form. It is not scientifically impossible for life to exist without an external designer, but a nearly infinite number of possibilities would need to happen by chance, rather like that tornado whipping up a working 747 jet from a junk heap. Of course, this still leaves the question of why the designer is not subject to these same physical laws, unless one assumes that the designer designed the physical laws as well.

The astronomer Sir Fred Hoyle calculated an extremely tiny probability for the spontaneous evolvement of a unicellular organism in our universe, given the chemical and physical raw materials available. Life would not exist unless organic chemicals first coalesced to become a unicellular organism. Beyond that, the burst of multicellular organisms appearing in the Cambrian geologic era happened much too fast for evolution alone to be the operator. Gerald Schroeder notes (Gerald L. Schroeder, 1997) that the number of gene mutations necessary for the diversity of multicellular organisms to develop without intervention would take hundreds of millions of years. Nonetheless, geological evidence tells us that the process took five million years. Unless directed or intended by an outside force, the timing is inconsistent with the materialist theory that assumes the process happened randomly. It is possible to flip an unbiased coin 100 times and get heads on every single flip, but the probability of this is tiny. Such is the case with these gene mutations. There simply was not enough time for randomness to allow multicellular organisms to form.

Although physics points in the direction of "intelligent design", I shrink from that term, since it has been used to describe a rather single-minded religious perspective that pretends to know more than the evidence provides. Using a term that has become entangled in religious politics is not an ideal term to provide evidence for why our universe exists and operates the way it does. Although the evidence from physics indicates an intelligent design of the universe, I have no desire to politicize or dogmatize the argument. When tiny probabilities unfolded into reality, it seems like magic, and that is fascinating in itself.

An early statistician studying thermodynamics, Ludwig Boltzmann, offered another scientific explanation for our unlikely universe, since our universe seems to have ignored its own law of entropy in order to exist in a tremendously unlikely state. (Boltzmann, p. 20) To be statistically possible without being prohibitively unlikely, our universe could be infinitely old. If so, it could have spent all but its most recent cosmological instant, which would be a few billion years, in an innumerably huge number of arrangements of disordered chaos. We just happen to be observing it during the miraculous instant in which it is ordered enough for galaxies and life to exist. During its vast existence of disorder, there would have been no one to observe it, since it was too disordered for life to form. We could only observe it if a miraculous exception to this rule has occurred. The problem with this theory is that the evidence points in a different direction, as science now accepts that our universe is not infinitely old, but began in an instant about 18 billion years ago. And this was the Big Bang, the dominant scientific theory of our universe's beginning, which harbors its own secrets—secrets that point to a universe that was designed rather than randomly cobbled together.

# CHAPTER

## 2

# DID ANYONE HEAR A BIG BANG?

THE DOMINANT AND ONLY WIDELY-HELD theory about the origin of our universe is the Big Bang, and it is supported by such overwhelming scientific evidence that it might be called a fact. Speaking of magic, the Big Bang itself is almost too improbable to have occurred without intention. Scientific data, grounded in the relative amounts of hydrogen and helium that exist, show that our universe began explosively from a single tiny point, from which all the galaxies emerged. Because of hydrogen's chemical valence and reactivity, there would be no more hydrogen in the universe had the universe existed in a steady state without the Big Bang.

Fred Hoyle originally coined the name "Big Bang", but he did so derisively. He considered it a pejorative term for a theory he felt to be steeped in the superstition of creation. Known for stellar nucleosynthesis, Hoyle originally was a materialist who never embraced the Big Bang theory despite strong evidence grounded in cosmic microwave background radiation. It was another piece of physics that made him conclude that our universe could not have been accidental. His analysis of carbon revealed that the window of resonance that would allow it to be formed was a virtual impossibility, and yet it is one of the primary building blocks of physical life. Despite his dismissive attitude toward creation stories, the abundance of carbon in our universe made an unlikely Hoyle come to the conclusion that the universe must have had a designer:

> Some super-calculating intellect must have designed the properties of the carbon atom; otherwise the chance of my finding such an atom through the blind forces of nature would be utterly minuscule. A common sense interpretation of the facts suggests that a super intellect has monkeyed with physics, as well as with chemistry and biology, and that there are no blind forces worth speaking about in nature. The numbers one calculates from the facts seem to me so overwhelming as to put this conclusion almost beyond question.
> --Fred Hoyle (Hoyle, November, 1981)

If that is not convincing enough to anyone embracing a random or accidentally formed universe, astrophysicist Brandon Carter noted in a 1974 paper referenced by Paul Davies in his book entitled *God and the New Physics*, that the probability that a star such as our sun exists is also insanely small. (Davies, 1983, p. 188) This is because the gravitational force, a fundamental constant of nature, places an upper and lower limit on allowable stellar masses. Science has revealed that an alteration in the strength of this gravitational force by as little as one part in 10 to the $40^{th}$ power would be all that would be necessary to imbalance the forces that allow a sun such as our own to exist. In case you are challenged by scientific notation, this means that an alteration of one part out of a number starting with 1 and followed by 40 zeroes occurs, the gravitational force would be too strong or too weak for our sun, and all stars in our universe would be either blue giants or red dwarfs. Consequently, all life that depends on yellow solar-type stars would have no environment allowing them to be here.

In this same vein, Roger Penrose in a 1979 article entitled "Singularities and time-asymmetry", noted that a random initial state of our universe after the Big Bang would mean that entropy would have created a universe of random disorder rather than stars and galaxies. The probability he estimated for our hospitable universe, as opposed to this? It is a mind-numbing 1 over 10 to the $10^{th}$ to the $30^{th}$ power (Penrose, 1979). Even if his estimate is off by a factor of a few trillion, the universe we live in appears to have been intended by a particularly precise design. Our sun does not implode into a black hole because of the enormous central pressure of its internal furnace. After lining up these startlingly small coincidences that allow us to exist as we do, the brilliant scientist Paul Davies wrote that "the seemingly miraculous concurrence of numerical values that nature has assigned to her fundamental constants must remain the most compelling evidence for an element of cosmic design." (Davies, 1983, p. 189)

To emphasize that there is scientific agreement on the tiny window for our universe's existence, one of physics' premier minds today made a similar point about the intensely unlikely possibility that our universe could survive its beginning. The aforementioned rate of expansion at the point of the Big Bang had already precluded the likelihood that it happened by chance. Although he does not specifically attribute this improbability to intentional design, Stephen Hawking nonetheless agrees that our universe as it exists is seemingly too improbable to exist.

> If the rate of expansion one second after the Big Bang had been smaller by even one part in a hundred thousand million million, it would have recollapsed before it reached its present size. On the other hand, had it been greater by a part in a million, the universe would have expanded too rapidly for stars and planets to form.
> --Stephen Hawking (Hawking, 1988)

Some scientists object to drawing conclusions from probabilities after an event has happened. Our universe is already here, and they say that, regardless of the astronomically small odds, we are witnessing one toss of the die. Although it may be that our toss resulted in the one chance in a gazillion to get a universe where the laws of physics allow life, it *could* happen without a miracle of design taking place. The statistician might balk at such an argument. A statistician's reluctance to accept the excruciatingly tiny possibilities for our universe is the same reluctance that does not accept the random formation of a working 747 by a tornado throwing junk around. The principle of Occam's razor has the better hand, in that relying on infinitesimally small probabilities is a far more complicated theory than assuming some kind of design.

"Everything is determined, the beginning as well as the end, by forces over which we have no control. It is determined for the insect, as well as for the star. Human beings, vegetables, or cosmic dust, we all dance to a mysterious tune, intoned in the distance by an invisible piper."

--Albert Einstein (Viereck, 1929)

# CHAPTER

# 3

# EINSTEIN'S SPOOKY ACTION AT A DISTANCE—THE ROOT OF PSI?

BEYOND STATISTICS ALONE, PHENOMENA THAT were thought to be superstitious are proving to be scientifically verifiable and are forcing open the doors that connect science and spirituality. Again, as science uncovers more layers of truth that defy statistical odds, the paranormal is poking its head into the scientific domain. First it became clear in the classic Michelson-Morley physics experiment that the act of observation determines whether light takes on the characteristics of a wave or a particle. Without observation, all light and electrons remain waves, only taking the form of particles when observed. This was an astounding crack in the concept of a mechanical universe, setting up the curious theory that *conscious observation* is the means for matter to be formed, again hinting at purposeful design.

On initially encountering the evidence for nonlocality and entanglement—which will be addressed in chapter 10—Albert Einstein, called it "goofy" and, in a letter dated March 3, 1947, refused to believe that quantum physics allowed for "spooky action at a distance" (Born, 1971). It has now been experimentally verified, and Einstein's comments are another example of how established notions of reality can become psychologically rigid even among visionaries, effectively stunting experimental research rather than opening doors. Although Einstein refused to believe that God was "playing at dice" (Born, 1971), research regarding Schrodinger's cat (which would allow a cat to be both simultaneously dead and alive depending on whether or not it had been observed), has shown that, metaphorically speaking, dice are indeed being played.

One of the criticisms of paranormal phenomena among traditional materialist scientists has been that paranormal energies are not electromagnetic energy, the form of energy that is measurable by physics. Recently however, Princeton's Boundary Institute found that there is a class of electronics that is affected by human consciousness, as people react to broadly-reported emotional events. Forty recording devices throughout the world have been operating around the clock since 1998, monitoring energy fluctuations after natural cataclysms or emotional events like the 9-11 tragedies (Braden, Speaking the Lost Language of God, 2003, p. 9). Likewise, magnetic fields have been discovered to respond to human emotions and feeling-based intentions, with the synchronous intention of a group of people producing greater responses than individuals alone. (Braden, Choice Point 2012: The Promise of our Future in the Cycles of the Past, 2010) Research at the HeartMath Institute in California has found that "individuals trained in feelings of deep love and appreciation are able to change the shape of their DNA" through intention (Braden, Speaking the Lost Language of God, 2003, p. 3). Likewise, fascinating research has determined that people with multiple personalities have eyeglass prescriptions that are different for different personalities, a profound example of mind over matter, since the physical characteristics of the eye's architecture would presumably remain the same regardless of which personality is in control an individual's psyche. Fifty years ago, such conclusions would never have been reported because such research would never have been done.

These connections may play a part in psychic communication. In physics, string theory allows for eleven dimensions of reality, in which much of what is considered psychic and paranormal could exist in the upper dimensions. The implications for psi of nonlocality in quantum mechanics have already moved beyond the realm of the hypothetical, after experiments regarding the instantaneous entanglement of atoms were performed and replicated. This would explain how psychic communication is effective and immediate, regardless of the distance between a sender and receiver.

Reality has a way of imposing itself in a way that trumps human beliefs. Einstein, Bohr, Heisenberg, and Schrodinger discovered that the physical universe is essentially non-physical and arises in a field that is even more subtle than energy—"a field that seems to be more like intelligence and consciousness than matter" (Randhawa, 2006, p. 2) This is a common meeting ground for science and metaphysics, as ancient metaphysical teachings have long held this to be the case. These new scientific discoveries are examples of science beginning to look more and more like spirit, with discoveries in quantum physics, nonlocality, and verified experiences rooted in out-of-body consciousness and near-death experiences. Indeed, the factual nature of science has morphed into what had previously been viewed as supernatural. Federico Faggin, the physicist known for designing the first commercial microprocessor, is now developing a physics of consciousness that is grounded in consciousness units rather than matter (Faggin, 2015). These shifts have been welcomed by some but are disquieting to scientists still looking for more traditional scientistic explanations.

William Tiller notes that "a long time ago we made the decision to separate spirit from science...so we were able to learn how to do science. But now we can take on the richer task of learning to do science when consciousness is part of the experiment" (Randhawa, 2006, p. 1). The field of cognitive neuroscience now strives to understand consciousness independently of brain structure, almost reversing the scientific perspective that still dominates mainstream thinking, which is to study consciousness by experimenting with the brain.

Until the late 19th century, the entire universe was hypothesized to be composed of an invisible substance known as the "aether", offering a model that allowed for the sharing of information through space. Curiously, in light of the metaphysical focus of this paper, the dominant theory was that aether (later spelled ether) was a material substance with a rather spiritual characteristic of connecting everything in the universe. The idea of a unified substance invisibly pervading everything and transferring information throughout the universe was long derided as infantile science, but new discoveries are making it look prescient.

The slippery concept of ether was eventually "disproved" by the Michelson and Morley experiment in 1887. I have italicized "disproved" because their experiment was unsophisticated, but the concept of the ether did not fit well in established science, so even a poorly designed experiment toppled it (Braden, Speaking the Lost Language of God, 2003) (CD 5). The experiment's weaknesses were overlooked because the scientific mindset was predisposed to believe that real science should not concentrate on eerie universal substances such as the indescribable ether. Rather, this mindset pushed science to focus on the properties of divisible, individual particles and waves.

Today we know that the initial scientific conception of an ether substance transporting information through the universe was certainly off-base, but the evidence of nonlocal energy and heart-based emotion today indicates that disposing of a medium of universal connection was a much too restrictive view of reality. The emerging view today of universal entanglement actually has vague similarities to the old aether, causing many scientists to re-form their beliefs to include a broader realm of bizarre realities that had been rejected as ridiculous. The ether concept may have appeared to fall off the edge of the earth, but it metaphorically has been found to be orbiting back into the scientific conception of universal consciousness. How ironic it would be if something akin to aether may yet be found to account for the transference of psychic information.

We first learn about the world through our senses and perceptions, and Newtonian physics was grounded in perceptual evidence as a form of proof, but experience and research have increasingly confirmed that perceptions cannot always be trusted. Perception told people that the earth was flat because human eyesight could not see far enough to see the earth's roundness, but a broader perspective revealed its round shape. The sun appeared to move around the earth rather than vice versa, which would be apparent if we could step out to see it from a wider perspective, but our perceptions work within a limited framework. Madame Marie Curie died from cancer that probably took root in working with radioactive substances and using early diagnostic X-rays on wounded soldiers, but because she felt no pain from radiation bombardment, she did not perceive that it was dangerous.

Since we cannot travel near the speed of light, we are deluded also by our tiny experience of motion. If I could board a ship traveling near the speed of light, any light moving in the same direction I am moving would still move away from me at the speed of light. My life experience tells me that this light should now be moving at nearly twice the speed of light (my speed plus its own speed), but this is a delusion of our limited perceptions. Our perceptions also delude us regarding time, again because our perspective is too small. Time seems to move constantly at the same rate, but human perception can only witness a tiny part of the spectrum of possibilities. We now have evidence from clocks on spaceships that Einstein's theory of special relativity is correct, that the pace of time's movement is dependent on how fast one is moving, up to the speed of light. This is so true that time stops completely for light, which creates the quirky reality that as long as light is traveling, no time passes for it. All continuously moving light is currently at the same instant of time as the Big Bang, as it has witnessed no change in time since the beginning of the universe. Yes, that is weird to our perception-based mentality, but yes, that is physics.

Invisible things, such as oxygen, exist where we live, so if oxygen suddenly disappeared, our perceptions alone probably could not identify the cause of our suffocation. Perception, a form of rapid thinking, is nothing more than a re-creation of reality in the mind, and more and more evidence exists that a mindset that "you'll see it when you believe it" is again revealed as more than a hopeful wish. (Dyer, You'll See It When You Believe It, 1989) Contradictions between science and spirit remain, but rather than seeing science and spirit as fundamentally different realities, it is now clear that the apparent contradictions are rooted in our perceptual inabilities and unwillingness to see the whole picture.

Because of complexity, science had broken down reality into minutia that could be studied individually, but this concentration on particles had blinded the scientific method, which has been a victim of its own limitations. The headwinds of a longstanding historic "scientistic" mindset are gradually changing, goaded by an emerging sense of urgency caused by overpopulation, global warming, stresses to obtain energy, and advances in technological warfare. It is becoming more clear that scientism is a degeneration of essential science "that harms many people by irrationally dismissing and pathologizing all aspects of the spiritual perspective". (Tart, 2009, p. 53) The need to include a spiritual dimension of reality is becoming too important to be overlooked, but fortunately, experimentation is revealing it.

Perhaps the entire universe, which is 15-18 billion light years across and full of so many stars that our numbering system is juvenile for enumerating them, may be like a grain of sand on a beach of universes. When the concept of location breaks down in quantum physics, it could be that the laws of one universe simply do not apply to the other universes. Science and spirit bring different points of view to the table, but the need for science to look within and seriously acknowledge such emerging realities leads it to converge more closely with spirit. Carried to their logical conclusion, new scientific findings and statistical probabilities simply make it more rational to believe in the "woo-woo" peculiarities of design than not to believe in them. It is still not proof, but the tables have turned for what is viewed as superstition and what is viewed as hard rationality.

# PART II

## THE REALITY OF PSI

# CHAPTER

## 4

# SCIENTISTIC RELUCTANCE

BEFORE EXPLORING THE EVIDENCE FOR psychic phenomena (psi), you may be wondering how we find ourselves in a society that mostly has overlooked the potential value of psychic tools. Cultural reluctance diminished the opportunity to reap the fruits of researching psi, even denying that it could possibly exist. We live in what Ann Jauregui calls an "achingly secular period in human history", where "there is not much support in our daily lives for the moments of revelation that arrive." (Jauregui, 2007, p. 29)

It was not always so. Societal knowledge grows in ways that take an anfractuous path to where we want to go. We follow a route that works well enough—until new information persuades us to change direction. Intellectuals largely accepted psychic phenomena as real until about the 1700s, when the Scientific Revolution introduced a new paradigm. Generally, this new rationalism was an improvement over unpredictable superstition, but it now appears that science followed this path too far and threw out the baby with the bathwater.

Scientists share in our human tendency to convert strongly held beliefs into entrenched ideology. And even after the initial reasons for embracing beliefs eventually give way to new discoveries, people are slow to let go of the dominant paradigm. Science's reductive materialism had become as intransigent as religious dogmatism, and ironically, scientists that perceived religion as superstition have been guilty of creating their own brand of dogmatic ideology. Charles Tart coined the term "scientistic" to describe this rather exclusionary scientific mindset (Tart, 2009, pp. 24-25), and although the word scientism has never made its way into the dictionary, perhaps it should. Tart argued that commonly held scientific beliefs can become psychologically rigid, whereby science ignores its own rules about the need for impartial experimentation when confronted with phenomena that depart from accepted notions of reality. I will borrow the word "scientism" as a shorthand reference for a closed scientific mindset that excludes culturally unacceptable psi phenomena from authentic scientific research. Once engrained, the religion of scientism rejects experimental evidence that conflicts with the prevailing view. Firmly maintaining entrenched modes of thinking certainly has kept the scientific study of psi suppressed. Materialistic determinism has been unwilling to accept the potential reality of energies that may not be material, although the notion of gravity forced its way through that barrier.

New theories must wait until the dominant paradigm can expand enough to absorb them. When the dominant paradigm encounters an anomaly that cannot be explained or explained away with the current worldview, pressure eventually forces the old way of thinking to change. But the process is slow. Anomalies from the established worldview initially are overlooked or viewed as an error. (Russell, 2002, p. 20) One of the most revealing historical examples of a reluctance to change is the medical evidence discovered by Ignaz Semmelweis, a nineteenth century Hungarian physician. In 1847, well before the germ research of Joseph Lister and Louis Pasteur, Semmelweis noticed that surgeons who washed their hands before surgery had fewer cases of post-operative puerperal fever complications than was typical for medical operations at the time. But since no theory existed to make sense of this pattern, some doctors were offended at the suggestion that they wash their hands before surgery. Physicians argued that washing hands sacrificed valuable time when surgery was imminently necessary. Semmelweis could only point to his experience that hand washing reduced puerperal fever in childbirth, from about 25 percent to 1 percent of the cases. He had the evidence of numbers, but he had no acceptable scientific explanation such as germ theory. Although he was highly ridiculed for his weird idea that contradicted the dominant mindset, Semmelweis pushed for the practice of hand washing based solely on his statistics. His rally for the crazy idea of washing hands insulted the premier surgeons of his day, and they wanted him out of the way. Semmelweis eventually was committed to an asylum, where he was beaten to death two weeks later by the guards (Semmelweis, Ignaz (1818-1865), 2013).

The statistical evidence for psi still confronts this type of problem today, as psychic impressions are real and accurate to a highly significant degree, but no theory for them fits within the dominant scientific paradigm. Naysayers belittle statistical evidence that supports psi. They argue that psychic researchers make an "assumption that any significant departure from the laws of chance in a test of psychic ability is evidence that something anomalous or paranormal has occurred...[thereby] assuming what they should be proving" (Carroll, 2011, p. 3). Doctor Semmelweis certainly found that statistical evidence for hand washing was not enough to fight an entrenched belief. I suggest that statistical significance alone should be enough to accept that psychic phenomena are real in some way, even if we have no theory to explain them adequately. Consider a culture that could use such expanded abilities to toast bread with mental powers alone. Archeologists have postulated that our scientific culture is the most advanced ever, since a toaster is a more advanced mechanical device than anything discovered in archeological digs of ancient cultures (Braden, Speaking the Lost Language of God, 2003). Yet Gregg Braden argues that such an attitude judges the advancement of culture from our own scientific paradigm. A culture that had the ability to toast bread by mental projection alone would likely be more advanced than one that developed a toasting machine and external power to do so. The accuracy of archeological conclusions, as in all science, is limited by the mindset we bring to the research. I believe it is unwise to ignore what the statistics are saying simply because we do not understand how psi phenomena operate, since there are fruits to be harvested by learning to use our psychic gifts.

Science still discounts the teachings of religions, indigenous spiritual traditions and anecdotal examples of psi. Although gradually opening up in the last few decades with new scientific discoveries that leave the previous tenets of accepted science rather dusty, a long road to the full acceptance and study of psi remains, so much so that the society at large is more open to psi than professional scientists. Recent survey data point out that "sixty percent of adult Americans believe in intuition, clairvoyance, and ESP", but "ninety-six percent of scientists from the National Academy of Sciences claim to be skeptics...." (Burnham, 2011) One consequence of this mindset is that colleges have been unsuccessful in gaining official accreditation for coursework in metaphysical and psychic fields from regional and national accrediting agencies in the United States and many other countries.

## ■ Sacrificing Psi on the Altar of Scientific Dogma

Although the evidence for the statistical existence of psychic phenomena is now overwhelming in research studies, its day- to-day impact in our lives is small. The reluctance to accept and act on these hokey research results is reflected in the response to genuine investigative work of the paranormal, such as research at the Institute of Noetic Sciences (IONS). IONS was instigated by astronaut Edgar

Mitchell (after a transcendental *satori* experience in space) and privately funded to address the gap between scientific research, global holistic spirituality, and paranormal phenomena. But because psychic phenomena arise and exist as a form of energy that is not electromagnetic and therefore outside the realm of our current scientific understanding, the Institute of Noetic Sciences bemoans that the same levels of statistical significance that are convincing in another area of science are not sufficient to satisfy academia when rooted in psychic phenomena (Radin D. P., 2013). Academic journals may choose not to present these statistically significant results on psi because they undermine accepted theories. Such roadblocks to the dissemination of information reflect an unscientific bias that favors accepted theories and thwarts our understanding and potential usage of psi (Caudill, 2012, p. 15) This reminds me of a tongue-in-cheek remark by Al Sharpton regarding results that lie outside commonly held beliefs: "That was a very well laid out, rational point. But I'll stick with my emotional opinion based on no facts or evidence." (Reissig, 2015)

Some institutions that have been accredited in other areas and work peripherally with psi actually seem reluctant to emphasize the paranormal nature of this research. The California Institute of Integral Studies, for instance, dabbles in the paranormal and offers degrees in various forms of psychology, mental health, and therapy within its School of Consciousness and Transformation, but it avoids offering formal degrees in metaphysical and or parapsychic fields (California Institute of Integral Studies, 2011). The University of Arizona experiments in paranormal consciousness research at its world-renowned Center for Consciousness Studies but avoids mentioning the paranormal or psychic among its published goals, tangentially wording its activities as "the study of consciousness and neighboring phenomena such as perception, emotion, and self-consciousness" (Center for Consciousness Studies, 2014). Such caution, though understandable, leaves psi in the shadows of scientific research.

It seems that religious institutions would seek to understand the paranormal, since miracles by definition lie outside the realm of perceptual explanation. But even some religious institutions contribute to the "hands off" nature of studying the metaphysical and paranormal. Some religious beliefs maintain that studies on the efficacy of prayer are "strictly beyond the reach of scientific investigation" (McTaggart 183). The ostensible argument is that studying such phenomena would be interfering with or wanting to act like God.

Ironically, the suppression of religion in the Soviet Union during the Communist era reduced this particular bias against studying the paranormal, and relatively more research on focused intention and prayer was done there than elsewhere. Elisabeth Targ, impressed by studies of distance-healing in the Soviet Union, noted that U.S. researchers often categorized distant healing as prayer, and once in this category, "it was officially declared out of bounds" (McTaggart, 2003, p. 183). These strict notions provided another example of the straightjacket imposed when science paradoxically preordained a tenet as false without researching it.

## We Are the Losers

We are paying a price for failing to study and tap the benefits of psi. The paucity of academic research on metaphysical and paranormal phenomena, broadly defined as near-death experiences, out-of-body experiences or astral projection, psychic abilities, psi, and mediumship has an indeterminate societal cost, since untold advancements may have accrued if we better understood these largely untapped resources.

One example would be the value of kinesiology in the courtroom. The late Dr. David Hawkins, a medical psychiatrist and consciousness researcher, claimed that the truth or falsehood of a statement could be determined with a simple test of arm strength, since his research showed a curious correlation between muscle strength and telling the truth. Most particularly, telling a lie temporarily weakened one's muscle strength. Hawkins theorized that an individual's consciousness is part of, and infused with, an all-encompassing field of universal knowledge. Each individual component of consciousness (including each of us) is a hologram that contains all the information of the whole (Hawkins D. R., 2005, pp. 11-52). As such, our consciousness can tap into the truth or falsehood of anything, and we are physically weakened when confronted with untruths and strengthened by truths. The individual need not be aware of the truth or falsehood of a statement for it to affect his or her muscle strength. Imagine the enormous opportunity-value, such as billions of dollars of legal costs and emotional suffering that could be avoided by a society having access to such a tool for distinguishing truth from falsehood, or integrity from criminal consciousness.

Hawkins' theory is one of many promising paranormal theories that could be tapped if seriously understood and employed, but because it is deemed as too hokey for genuine researchers with reputations to uphold, it is unfunded and remains a simple statistical correlation. In my personal life, I could have used an arm strength test when I recently hired a contractor to repair a problem with my house, as it is notoriously difficult to distinguish true integrity from crooks who are great actors. This contractor looked and spoke honorably when he told me that he sincerely needed my last payment so that he could purchase materials to finish my job the next day. I asked what guarantee I had that he would finish my job if I gave him the last payment, he said "You have my word." "I hope it's more than words," I said, and he again assured me that the work would be done to my satisfaction. I reluctantly gave him the payment for the materials, and despite my efforts and contacts with the organization that recommended him, the job was left half completed and I have never seen or heard from him again. I recently discovered that he is "on the run" to avoid felony charges. Imagine the value of ascertaining the integrity of a person with a simple test of arm strength. The legal profession might balk at the loss of work in determining true facts, but their investigative tasks could be streamlined and our justice system improved.

In the world of medicine, a tragic reality of reductive materialist thinking is that we overlook unorthodox medical possibilities that appear impossible from our scientific perspective, consequently short-circuiting potential solutions and prolonging unnecessary suffering. One exceptional example was relayed by Gregg Braden, who personally witnessed communal healing of bladder cancers by Chi-lel Qigong in a "medicineless" hospital in Beijing, China (Braden, Speaking the Lost Language of God, 2003, p. 8 (CD)). Traditional medical science had determined that these cancers were no longer operable and relegated these hopelessly terminal cases to the medicineless hospitals, where purely spiritual methods of healing were employed. Braden has video evidence of spontaneous healings of inoperable cancers, based on "heart-based" meditative healing. He shared these videos with Western cancer researchers, who were amazed by the number and speed of spontaneous healings they witnessed. I will visit this issue later, but for now, the use of limited research funds to study the healing possibilities of this feeling-based thought prayer had no place within the western medical mindset, so getting research funding was circumvented at the starting gate.

In yet another arena, stories of time dilation have been swept aside as impossible, even while documentation effectively has proved that it is happening. One intriguing example occurred to a group of inspired individuals on a bus traveling to the Egyptian pyramids. The bus arrived at the pyramids in an impossibly short time, when an eight-hour trip was completed in four hours on one occasion, despite being stopped more often than usual. Gregg Braden documented that the bus driver insisted they could not be where they were, since they had arrived at their destination in half the usual time and the trip was otherwise normal ((Braden, Speaking the Lost Language of God: Awakening the Forgotten Wisdom of Prayer, Prophecy and the Dead Sea Scrolls, 2003). Similarly, Sonia Choquette and a friend reported driving through central Nebraska on a snowy evening, having a near accident when someone suddenly appeared in the center of the road, and finding themselves very soon afterward at a location forty miles outside Denver, Colorado. She has time-stamped receipts from a gasoline fill-up in central Nebraska to document that the two of them simply could not have driven as far as Colorado in the amount of time that had passed (Choquette, Your Psychic Pathway: Listening to the Guiding Wisdom of your Soul, 1993). If such events are too weird for the scientific paradigm, they are dismissed as hallucinations or fakery. Serious research about what is going on gets swept aside, leaving us no wiser in understanding the underlying phenomena.

Another example of nascent research that has been circumvented with a cynical eye was the work of Rupert Sheldrake, an English biochemist and plant physiologist. Sheldrake researched morphogenesis, the biological process of how organisms get their shape, and found intriguing evidence of morphic fields that may affect and guide human and animal development. These fields appear to share memories and could explain why training animals in a skill increases the ability of subsequent animals to learn that skill, even if these two groups of animals never come in contact with each other. Morphic resonance could be related to telepathy, precognition, scopaesthesia (the nonvisual sense of knowing when one is being stared at), and the ability of canines to know when their owners are coming home from a trip, but the problem once again was that these morphic theories did not fit the accepted scientific paradigm. The field got passed off as pseudoscience, discouraging serious researchers from pursuing further understanding of its correlations and any potential benefits (Burnham, 2011, p. 12).

# CHAPTER

# 5

# HOW WE GOT IN THIS RUT:
# A WALK THROUGH HISTORY
# OF THE PARANORMAL

HISTORY IS INFORMATIVE ABOUT HOW we arrived at this jaundiced academic view of paranormal phenomena. If you are itching to get on with the juicy evidence, I invite you to skip this chapter. But if you are a history buff or someone who simply yearns to understand why psychics are still considered hokey and weird, this chapter is for you.

Western science found its roots in sweeping away the supernatural beliefs of an uneducated and undisciplined population during the medieval historical period. Until the Renaissance, science was dominated by alchemy, astrology, and mystical explanations, and in the writings of Isaac Newton, there was no distinction made between science and spirit, allowing both materialistic and God-directed explanations for the existence and behavior of the physical world. The world and heavens were understood to behave by rules grounded largely in the philosophy of Aristotle and Plato, but there was also an accepted acknowledgement that an unpredictable randomness was at play.

Isaac Newton, whose classical physics became the linchpin of scientific thinking, was far less of a materialist than those who later embraced his theories. Profoundly religious, Newton wrote that the cosmos was infused with God and that gravity was a "divine energy" (Jauregui, 2007, p. 57). He believed that his laws described how God worked in our world and noted that his law of gravity should be interpreted as more than a mechanism when he wrote:

> This most beautiful system of the sun, planets, and comets, could only proceed from the counsel and dominion of an intelligent Being. [...] This Being governs all things, not as the soul of the world, but as Lord over all. [...] The Supreme God is a Being eternal, infinite, [and] absolutely perfect.
>
> (Thayer, 1953, p. 42)

It is ironic that the father of our materialistic view of the world was far more spiritual in his cosmology than the realm of classical physics that we inherited from him. Some of Newton's writings would today be categorized as studies of the occult, and some of his private notes could be interpreted as a prophecy of a quantum universe. He wrote that the world was virtually empty of matter, a prescient statement that found verification in the twentieth century. This brilliant man was responsible for the classical laws of motion and gravity and instrumental in the development of calculus, and had developed an integrated cosmology that was subsequently attacked with the very mechanical theories he had developed. His notes about Nature as a living Chaos read more like a sacred hint at today's quantum physics than the pared-down mechanistic physics he was induced to publish. As Newton's laws of motion and gravity became institutionalized in a learned world weary of religious persecution, social pressures caused Newton to sift out religious descriptions from his writings, leaving his physical laws as bare-bones descriptions. This new era of rationalism was far preferable to the fanaticism of the Inquisition. These attacks aimed at maintaining a secular order and flow of funds led him to expunge the spiritual from what were largely mystical and hermetic explanations. Curiously, Newton himself was the first victim of the materialistic paradigm which is attributed to him.

The Renaissance and the Age of Enlightenment welcomed a perspective less manipulated by those with political or religious power. Intellectuals were eager to inspire a natural philosophy that gave answers free of randomness, politics, and religious authority. The time was ripe for a materialistic, or reductionist, mindset to challenge a supernatural one. In astronomy, observation took precedence over philosophical conjecture. With the advent of telescopes, actual observations were answering confusing questions about planetary motion, so with Copernicus in the 16th century, followed by Galileo, Kepler, and Newton, something very valuable was taking root in astronomy and physics. That was predictability. Unpredictable consequences grounded in the supernatural unknown had been a source of fear that impeded progress. The new physics showed that the same causes always had the same effects, giving a newfound capacity to know what would happen when we harness motion and jiggle with the physical world.

Increasing the predictability of events was a huge improvement over randomness, so science was intentionally separating itself from the supernatural. The Scientific Revolution was revising the way that intellectuals described the world, with the dominant perspective moved away from viewing everything as a living entity and collapsed everything down to a mechanized piece of clockwork. An ability to replicate experiments and make accurate predictions about how this mechanical world works was a hallmark of scientific achievement that made people less threatened by a capricious world. But this also made psi the object of suspicion. Psi was incompatible with this new materialism because psi had no known physical explanation. Some early scientists were also motivated by a desire to avoid religious persecution and gain some liberation from the political power of the church (Callahan, 2005, p. 1).

In this new world of the materialist, it was believed that everything should be explained in terms of electrical currents and chemical and physical reactions. When these were unknown, it simply meant that the operative physical laws had yet to be discovered. As Isaac Newton found in his initial writings, references to God's actions were becoming viewed as evasive at best and discouraged from acceptable scientific discourse, causing him to tone down the spiritual descriptions of his physical laws (Snobelen, 2011). If an occult event could not be explained with the tools available, it was likely ignored in preference for something that could be observed and subjected to experimentation. The mind and spirit become mere epiphenomena, so psychic phenomena were dismissed as something philosophical, supernatural, and unreal. And if they were not real, they were not worthy of scientific study (Tart, 2009, p. 70). With this cultural hangover, only units of matter became "valid components of truly scientific discourse" (Westfall, 1977, p. 31).

Advances of science initially pointed toward animal and human life as something that could be distilled down to tiny individual components. In the material world, everything must be reducible to particles, matter, and force fields such as atomic forces, gravity, and magnetism. If it could not be explained in this way, its purported existence was assumed to be grounded in superstition, fraud or deception. Physical life was equated with mechanics, following a belief that human and animal behavior could be predicted precisely if all the material components were known. Bertrand Russell remarked that humanity was an accidental collocation of atoms doomed to extinction in the vast death of the solar system. He argued that no heroism or intensity of thought or feeling could preserve an individual life beyond the grave, and that this "fact" was "so nearly certain that no philosophy that rejects [it] can hope to stand" (Russell, 2002, pp. 6-7). The more that science isolated places in the nervous system that correlated with sight, hearing, and thought, materialists such as Bertrand Russell used the results to say that science and religion, rather than being complementary, stood in contradiction. In academia, the attitude was becoming calcified that science was hands-on while spirituality was philosophy at best and, at worst, an unreal fantasy grounded in ignorance, fear, and superstition.

This tendency to impose predetermined boundaries to accepted scientific research had been labeled "scientific imperialism" by John Dupre, as he argued that such a mindset generally suffers decreasing success the more it is embraced (Dupre, 2001, p. 16). As an example, one aspect of the new mechanical philosophy was to create models, and as ideological rigidity in the use of this method took hold, it was more important to have a model—any model—than to have a realistic model (Callahan, 2005, p. 1). Magnetism, for example, was a thorny issue to explain, so its explanations had traditionally been rooted in the occult. Following the emerging trendiness of mechanical models, Descartes devised a magnetism model in which magnetic bodies emitted streams of little screw-shaped particles that drew other objects toward it. Today, this is weirder than accepting psychic phenomena as scientific, but it was taken seriously because it fit within the accepted scientific method of the time.

## ■ Fraud and Gullibility Played a Role

For many people, the word "psychic" still elicits a Halloweenesque mental image of a woman with huge earrings, a bizarre headdress, and long, curly fingernails. For some reason, the psychic is almost always portrayed as a woman. She is peering into a crystal ball and can be expected to use sleight-of-hand tactics in a darkened room to trick gullible clients. What psychic abilities she has are grounded in trickery and magic, which is to say that she has no genuine psychic ability at all. This image has been pervasive and true to a degree that fraud was a fundamental reason that society rejected the possibility of true paranormal and psychic activity. Psychic shows rarely had anything to do with real psychic phenomena, but they became society's main exposure to the field. So, social convention came to view psi as occult trickery carried out by charlatans and entertainers hijacking it to earn a livelihood. Mostly entertainers drew on magician's tricks to achieve the appearance of something metaphysical, so the obvious result was that the reputation of psychic and paranormal phenomena suffered almost fatally.

Richard Hodgson, a secretary of the American Society for Psychical Research in the late nineteenth century, lamented this state of affairs and because of faith in his own psychic experiences, sought to overcome this sordid perception. He and Harry Price resolved to uncover fraud among spiritualist mediums of his day. Hodgson aimed to trap those who were not authentic, taking the role of a "hammer of cheats". He unmasked frauds such as Eusapia Palladino, discovered the use of trapdoors in psychic fairs, and even found trickery used by the widely heralded Madame Blavatsky. But his work backfired. Rather than exposing and rooting out the frauds, his efforts ironically focused society's limelight on the worst "psychic" practitioners (Hodgson, 2011), and as a result, the public became even more convinced that trickery trumped the authentic in the realm of the psychic and paranormal.

In the academic world, opinions about the metaphysical were further harmed by disingenuous psychic research during World War II, particularly the Soal-Goldney experiments on precognitive ability in 1941 through 1943. The studies had been well regarded by serious researchers and those interested in the potential war-time applications of psychic tools, but independent checking and witnesses revealed that Dr. Soal had altered some of his raw data to improve his success rate, and his cheating further poisoned the atmosphere for psi research (Markwick, 1978). Later, in the early 1970s, a number of experiments on extrasensory perception by Walter J. Levy, director of the Institute of Parapsychology, also were found to be fraudulent and extensively reported as such (Stefko, 2009).

The reputation of psi was already seriously damaged, but the vocal critic James Randi decided it needed to be put to rest for good. Although he himself was an entertainer rather than a bona fide researcher, Randi received enough publicity to further drive a wedge between psi and what little respectability it maintained. He engineered an effort called Project Alpha, which was an attempt to show that psi researchers were predisposed to expect a particular positive outcome before their research was undertaken. In Project Alpha, two young magicians deceived experimenters who had been tricked to believe that sham demonstrations were authentic psychic abilities, which made the researchers look gullible. The hoax by Randi fueled an increasingly skeptical world to discredit research on the paranormal. That was ironic, given that Randi's intentions preordained that his own experiments would be far from pure and unbiased. Randi had helped found the Committee for the Scientific Investigation of Claims of the Paranormal, which expressly stated that all psychic phenomena were falsely engineered. It published the *Skeptical Inquirer*, which repeatedly resorted to name-calling and ridicule to belittle parapsychology (Irwin, An Introduction to Parapsychology, 1989, pp. 272-274).

A more recent example of the societal headwinds facing authentic psychic research involved psychologist Gary Schwarz, who waded into a professional minefield by attempting to use the scientific method to study psychic mediumship. He designed a scientific study of the abilities of John Edward, a medium whose popular television show made him a highly visible and celebrated example of mediumship. Edward welcomed the chance to have his abilities analyzed, since he bemoaned that "people refer to me as a 'freak' or 'fraud'" (Schwartz G. E., The Sacred Promise: How Science is Discovering Spirit's Collaboration with Us in Our Daily Lives, 2011, p. xii). Edward said that his mediumship "needed an academic scholar to shed some much-needed light and credibility... and take [his mediumship from] a parlor trick and something that only fools believe in to a place where it sparks conversations and personal growth" (Schwartz G. E., The Sacred Promise: How Science is Discovering Spirit's Collaboration with Us in Our Daily Lives, 2011).

Schwarz undertook the study and reported statistically significant results. But instead of an academic peer review of his methodology and results, an organization intent on discrediting the study took center stage. The Committee for Skeptical Inquiry's Ray Hyman, a critic of parapsychology, wrote a critique of Schwartz's methodology and conclusions in an issue of the *Skeptical Inquirer.* Schwarz followed the one-sided attack with his own defense paper, and in a carnival atmosphere of emotionally charged claims and counter claims, any chance of a serious academic critique had clearly been trumped by bias and innuendo.

This same Ray Hyman was confronted with powerful evidence for remote viewing (psychically sensing the geography or events at a distant location), in a study conducted by the U.S. military. Hyman admitted that the military's evidence was extremely strong and that he could not find a flaw in the experimental protocol. Nonetheless, he refused to endorse it. Scientist Maureen Caudill wrote that Hyman "concluded without any firm basis that the remote viewing *must* have flaws because otherwise they'd mean psychic skills are real, and he simply didn't believe that could be true." (Caudill, 2012, p. 161)

Although professional psychics are attempting to employ their abilities with integrity, true psi has its authenticity and reputation sullied by those whose legitimacy is trumped by economic opportunism. Much scientific and social criticism is legitimate because what passes for psi in our culture includes a hefty helping of garbage. Unfortunately, much of this garbage is promulgated by undisciplined believers who loosely accept anything psychic as legitimate. Personally, I do not trust many "professional" psychics and am somewhat embarrassed by the lack of questioning among some proponents of psi. It may be revealing that I have never had a reading myself from a professional psychic, and this reluctance arises from my suspicion about the authenticity of many of them. I find psychic fairs to be rather frothy and unsubstantial, as they often display a lack of self-restraint in an atmosphere that accepts too much and questions too little. These fairs certainly have their serious and integrous practitioners, but they generally include monetary entertainment events that belie the real value of psi and thwart legitimate and serious research in the field.

For instance, I find that the evidence for the energy efficacy of crystals appears to be grounded in subjective psychological states. I do not deny that subjective psychological beliefs can be effective. I actually believe that wholeheartedly, given the successful research on the efficacy of placebos, and I am open to the possibility that crystals may contain inherent energies that are not understood. But if such energies exist, that form of energy currently remains outside our capacity to study them scientifically and harness their value. So regarding crystals, I am guilty of perpetuating the same attitude that I am criticizing. Overall, however, I strive to remain open-minded about all areas of psi and the paranormal, but I simply believe that stooping to wishful thinking besmirches the reputation of serious research that already suffers a shaky reputation in the scientific community. This allows serious science, in looking at psi, the excuse to ignore what is real, effectively throwing the baby out with the bath water.

## ▓ The Headwinds of Denial

. . . . . . . . . . . . . . . . . . . . . . . . . . . . . . . . . . . . . . . . . . . . . . . . . . . . . . .

I already mentioned that 60 percent of American adults agreed with the statement that "some people possess psychic powers or ESP" and that the percentage that believes in extrasensory perception has increased from polls taken about twenty years earlier (Radin D., Entangled Minds, 2006, p. 38). Of the various possible interpretations of this trend, the U.S. National Science Foundation chose to report that these poll results reflected ignorance, focusing on the increasing percentage over time as evidence of the "deplorable state of science education in the United States" (Ibid.).

In musing over the potentially negative impact of such perceptions, Charles Tart bemoaned that "Modern science...declares seekers or the spiritually inclined, at best, [to be] softheaded folks who are wasting their time because they're unwilling to be properly scientific in their view of what is and isn't real and, at worst, superstitious fools, probably with serious stupidity or psychopathology...." (Tart, 2009, p. 19). Noting the roadblock implications of scientific materialism to understanding and benefiting from the paranormal, Tart went so far as to claim that scientism is a "dogmatic corruption" of science, resulting in continued scientific ignorance of the causes and reasons for paranormal events.

Raymond Moody, the professor who published the first serious research on near-death experiences (NDEs), provided a good example of this. He ran into a wall of resistance from those who maintained that anything real would already have been researched, a catch-22 that unstudied paranormal phenomena are not believed because they have never been seriously studied. When Moody first shared his analysis of near-death experiences with medical doctors, many initially were convinced that had NDEs been true, they already would have encountered such information in their medical training (Moody, 2001). This sense of believing that the professional literature would surely be awash with reports on anything real is similar to my own consternation and surprise about Silva Mind Control at the beginning of this book. Had its claims to improve one's psychic abilities been real, one surely would expect it to have been addressed in academic psychology classes. The doctors coming across Moody's lone research were saying it must be quackery because it was not already acknowledged in medical literature. A lack of research keeps science adolescent in the paranormal arena and maintains the mindset that has kept it that way. Likewise, quality researchers and educators avoid the field because it is professionally risky to research an illusory field, and it remains illusory because there has been too little research to verify its reality.

The tragedy then is that the lack of serious research precludes the harnessing of knowledge it may offer. There is tandem resistance to formalizing education to include paranormal phenomena (McTaggart, 2003, pp. 224-227). Paranormal events are happening, but they are passed off as anomalies rather than investigated with limited resources and included in education curricula. Confronted with these studies, some critics still claim that statistical evidence is not proof of psi but is merely interpreted as such.

Even though serious research was all but nonexistent, the U.S. National Academy of Sciences said in 1988 that there is "no scientific justification from research conducted over a period of 130 years for the existence of parapsychological phenomena" (Druckman, 1988, p. 22). There may have been little research, but this pronouncement from a respected scientific authority had a powerful consequence of further weakening fundamental research in paranormal and psychic areas. The field was now more than unfunded, but exorcised as unworthy of serious consideration for funding. Professional status concerns and the desire of researchers to be respected by their peers, tied with the need to maintain a reputation for the sake of earning a livelihood, now made it more difficult for those interested in studying the paranormal from doing so. This admittedly practical response continues to put up roadblocks to a better understanding of these "meta" and "para" fields of research.

Consequently, contemporary parapsychological research actually waned in the United States from the 1980s until just recently. Many university laboratories working in this field in the United States had closed, often citing a lack of acceptance by mainstream science (Odling-Smee, 2007, p. 10). For example, Robert Jahn, an applied physics professor, had earned a distinguished reputation in plasma dynamics at Princeton when he inherited a study aimed at determining the effect of consciousness on random number generators. To conduct the research, he set up a small program with a neutral name: the Princeton Engineering Anomalies Research Laboratory (PEAR). The program was never allotted much respect and was relegated to a few rooms in a basement at Princeton University. According to Lynne McTaggart, Princeton tolerated PEAR "largely because of Jahn's reputation", "like a patient parent with a precocious but unruly child" (McTaggart, 2003, p. 112). Despite some highly significant statistical results regarding paranormal research, PEAR ceased operations in 2007.

U.S. educational institutions are not accredited for professional programs in metaphysical fields. Here again is a "chicken or egg" cycle where progress is stymied because research by unaccredited institutions is viewed as suspect because of their lack of professional credentials. With monetary and theoretical challenges to studying psi, accredited U. S. universities currently involved in such endeavors still have names that disguise or underplay the parapsychological/ metaphysical nature of the metaphysical branch of research, such as the Division of Perceptual Studies in the Department of Psychiatry and Neurobehavioral Sciences at the University of Virginia and the Center for Consciousness Studies at the University of Arizona. The Institute of Parapsychology at Duke University, which coined the term Extrasensory Perception (ESP), is now the Rhine Research Center. Although it still publishes the Journal of Parapsychology, the Rhine's name reveals little about its research since 1927 on telepathy, clairvoyance, and precognition. The California Institute of Integral Studies conducts incidental paranormal research as a part of its Consciousness Studies program, which remains a name that gives little hint of anything paranormal. Research on remote viewing was once common at the Stanford Research Institute, but war was the impetus for study there, aimed at matching or exceeding the success of remote viewing work in the Soviet Union. When military funding dried up after the cold war, this paranormal study on the Stanford campus virtually ceased. Excellent research initiated by Dr. Ian Stevenson and continued by Dr. Bruce Greyson on children remembering past lives is ongoing at the University of Virginia School of Medicine, but it is housed under an unfortunate name that does not reveal this angle—the Division of Perceptual Studies. A few foundations include the Parapsychology Foundation in New York City and Greenport, New York, the Alvarado Zingrone Institute for Research and Education (Theozire.org), and, of course, The Institute of Noetic Sciences (IONS).

Of more than 3,000 colleges and universities, less than 1 percent host faculty that publically admit to interest in psi research (Radin D., Entangled Minds, 2006, p. 280). The amount of research funds spent on the paranormal worldwide remains miniscule. If the amount raised worldwide for cancer research was spent in a 24-hour day, what has been spent on psi research throughout history would equal a mere 43 seconds of cancer expenditures (Radin D., 2006, p. 278).

Although the scientific materialist paradigm is globally pervasive, the professional arena for parapsychological and paranormal research is somewhat more accepting in the British Isles than in the United States, and this is reflected in a greater willingness to support paranormal research under names that represent the work being done. British paranormal research programs include the Koestler Parapsychology Unit in its Department of Psychology at the University of Edinburgh, Northampton's Center for the Study of Anomalous Psychological Processes, the Russell Grant College of Psychic Studies, and Liverpool Hope University's Transpersonal Psychology Research Unit. Still, the United Kingdom has not been untouched by resistant thinking. Henry Sidgwick, a professor at Cambridge and first president of the Society for Psychical Research, lamented way back in 1882 how "scandalous" it was "that a dispute as to the reality of [psi] phenomena was still going on" (Radin D., Entangled Minds, 2006, p. 279).

The winds of change finally favor a more open approach to researching psi, and a nascent recovery is underway in the last few years. The focus to date has been proving that the phenomena are real, but more than statistical "proof" is necessary to make it useful. Discovering what underlies the statistical reality remains. Not only are psychic impressions often very subtle and subject to error, but we have no conclusive theory that explains what they are. Scientists have habitually denied or ignored the paranormal for this reason, noting that their primary objection is not being able to explain what is going on. Science would be more likely to accept the statistical evidence that psi exists if they knew *how* it exists. This is all the more crucial since whatever psi is, it appears to lie outside the traditional scientific paradigm, which is still fundamentally based in materialism, atomic forces, gravity, and electromagnetic energy—and psi simply does not appear to fit into any of these boxes.

# CHAPTER
## 6

# CAN PSI BE UNDERSTOOD SCIENTIFICALLY?

P.M.H. ATWATER, WHO RESEARCHED NEAR-DEATH experiences for 33 years, implies that the laboratory is a poor environment to study the paranormal. Atwater pointed out that her research actually broadened her understandings of how science could be performed. "Experience had long taught me that transformational shifts in consciousness and the wide sweep of exceptions that can occur because of them were outside the range of double-blind studies with a control group" (Atwater, Near-Death Experiences: The Rest of the Story, 2011). In a nutshell, to be convincing, the study of the paranormal requires something beyond traditional statistical research.

Jeffrey Kripal, a professor of Religious Studies at Rice University, agrees. "Whatever paranormal events are, they did not evolve so that a bored sophomore can look at playing cards and try to send an abstract shape to another bored sophomore. They are about...something else" (Dow, 2010, p. 20). Within current scientific knowledge, laboratory settings for studying the paranormal are trying to capture something both experientially real and simultaneously unreal in the realm of current academic thinking. "We have no way of explaining them with our present materialist or subjectivist models." (Dow, 2010)

As such, it could be argued that western science simply does not know how to do research on the paranormal phenomena of psychic abilities known as psi. If psi exists in a different reality altogether, physics and the scientific method may be the wrong tools to study it. If the psychic and paranormal are rooted in what quantum physics calls entanglement, how can instantaneous connections outside the flow of time be studied? Consider the simple inability of the scientific method to study the power of prayer, in which one control group will be prayed for and one will not be prayed for. Even ignoring the fundamental nature of prayer, it is simply not possible to have pure control groups since researchers cannot keep people from praying for those in the "not-to-be-prayed-for" group.

David Hawkins' consciousness map offers an explanation for the difficulty of trying to use scientific investigation to study paranormal phenomena. Hawkins developed a logarithmic scale on which consciousness could be measured, and the scale ranged from 0 to 1,000. A level of 1,000 matches the highest level achievable in a human body, a level Hawkins equated with Christ consciousness. Levels calibrating below 200 represent a consciousness that lacks integrity and is exemplified by states of despondency, alienation, and destruction. When Hawkins calibrated scientific thought, he found that it tops out at a level of 499, while levels of 500 and above are in a realm where rational thought gives way to spirituality (Hawkins D., 1995, p. 223) According to Hawkins, the reason that science is not the appropriate tool for studying the paranormal is that the consciousness levels of science do not overlap with those of spirituality, resulting in a break between different realms. If Hawkins is correct, it would not be possible to research spiritual dimensions with tools from a different level of consciousness.

Thinking of this conceptually, one could not completely measure love on a numerical scale, where the totality of the concept is diminished by reducing it to a measurement that does not capture its full essence. Attempting to measure the paranormal with instruments grounded in a scientific mindset may be like attempting to measure speed or height with a bathroom scale. The method of measurement is not appropriate to capture the fundamental nature of what is being analyzed.

Orthodox scientists are puzzled and made skeptical about the paranormal because they lack a working theory such as electromagnetism to explain it. Some type of energy is operating, but what kind? Dr. W. G. Roll, president of the Parapsychological Association postulated as early as 1964 that there are "psi fields" that are analogous to electromagnetic or gravitational fields (Tompkins, 2002, p. 58) Psi fields and thought itself are clearly energetic, but this energy is a different sort of energy than current physics can address and understand. Dr. G. D. Wasserman leans on quantum mechanics and inconceivably small quanta to explain psychic fields (Tompkins, 2002). Recent explanations call on a universal holographic nature of reality, in which each part of the universe contains the information of the whole. This universal interconnectedness allows for instantaneous sharing of information without need for the time it takes to transmit information, effectively violating the theory that nothing can travel faster than the speed of light. Just as electromechanical energy was not measurable in the past, yet was eventually comprehended, the lack of understanding about the psychic and paranormal might be explained as immature science that is not advanced enough to recognize a different form of valid energy. "Separations that we see between ordinary, isolated object are...illusions created by our limited perceptions...and connected in ways we're just beginning to understand" (Radin D., Entangled Minds, 2006, p. 14).

Even in an environment that does not know how to conduct research on the totality of psi, abundant statistical evidence that psychic phenomena exist has been generated. The Global Consciousness Project at Princeton University is awash with highly statistically significant studies of psychic intuition (IONS Conference, 2009), even though there remains very little operative understanding of what is going on. One common study included four distinct pictures. A sender was assigned a picture and asked to concentrate on it. A receiver at a separate location was asked to determine which of the pictures the sender was thinking about. Chance would expect a correct "hit" rate of one in four, or 25 percent, but the observed rate averaged 32 percent correct. Princeton's Global Consciousness Project provided the opportunity for such studies to be undertaken widely around the world, and the number of studies by different researchers was so huge that the odds of averaging 32 percent correct without psi was one in one trillion (Radin D., Supernormal, 2013, p. 191). A couple of skeptical researchers sought to debunk the results but, interestingly, found 32 percent correct in their own research. Not surprisingly, they were reluctant to attribute this to psi and reported that the result "was precariously close to demonstrating [that] humans do have psychic powers" (Howard, 2005, p. 298). Thirty-two percent is the average correct percentage at this task for the general public, but meditators have a vastly better rate of accuracy, picking the correct picture about 50 to 55 percent of the time (Radin D., 15th International Conference of the Institute of Noetic Sciences, 2013). Even without understanding the underlying mechanism, the statistics show that something **is** going on, buttressed by intriguing but common anecdotal experiences that beg to be understood. Ignoring or denying them *a priori* actually violates the scientific method's reliance on experimentation and replication.

Consciousness research that transcends the materialist mindset—such as research on whether consciousness arises outside the brain—is also caught in the maelstrom of acceptable borders for research funding and the befuddlement about how to do it. Although the societal perspective has broadened, most scientists still assume that consciousness arises from the brain, despite metaphysical experiences that cannot be explained by this paradigm. Traditional science theorizes that consciousness emerged during evolution as a by-product of complex computation among brain neurons, arguing that neurons and synapses are akin to bit states and switches in computers. This view pays a price that requires consciousness to be a helpless spectator merely along for a ride with the body and disappearing after the body dies. Neurocomputation precludes the possibility of non-local conscious phenomena such as often-reported out-of-body and astral projection experiences, backward time effects, near-death experiences, events witnessed during neocortical shutdown, and feelings of connection to a deeper reality. These paranormal phenomena suggest a much broader reality, implying that the theory of neurocomputation is incomplete and that consciousness may have existed all along as an intrinsic part of the universe, in accord with ancient writings. This view had been considered unscientific until recent discoveries in quantum physics, where concepts such as nonlocality (instantaneous connections between widely separated particles) are potentially bringing these ancient ideas back into the realm of science. A 2011 consciousness conference in Sweden seriously addressed how to tackle these issues from a scientific perspective (Studies, 2011, p. 1).

Quantum physics is deeply entrenched in our understanding of physics today and it opens doors for the scientific research of the paranormal. Through the process of experimentation, conjecture, and mathematical rigor, quantum mechanics has brought science right to the door of psi, potentially providing a theoretical basis for its existence. Quantum mechanics began with the work of an exceedingly traditional scientist, the German physicist, Max Planck, tackling an exceedingly down-to-earth problem. Planck was researching the peculiar dilemma of why hot objects glow red. His work, in conjunction with Einstein's first paper on the photoelectric effect, brought physics to a discovery that seemed rather magical and hard to believe—that light is made up of tiny packets of energy.

Because these packets, or quanta, only came in discrete amounts, light is not continuous. Instead, it is only available in unitized packets like the steps on a ladder. One could have 2 or 3 units of light, for example, but 2-1/2 is impossible. Traditional physicists at the time did not want to accept this, as Newton's physics allowed light to have any energy level. Planck and Einstein effectively showed that waves of light have the properties of particles and in a subsequent piece of research by Louis de Broglie, particles of matter were kooky enough to have the properties of waves.

Now, this was weird, but reducing the mathematical and theoretical complexity to a simple conclusion, physics was hinting at a world in which everything is one. Matter and fields of waves shared the same properties. Energy and matter were the same things, distinguished only by different frequencies. We already knew that the apparent separations of solid matter, such as my hand and a table having solid boundaries, is akin to that illusion that makes the spinning blades of a fan look solid, but quantum theory was now saying that everything is ultimately composed of the same quantum stuff. We are by no means at a point where physicists agree on quantum theory, which remains a model of the universe in mathematical terms, but if you want an excellent discussion on the various interpretations, take a look at Nick Herbert's book entitled *Quantum Reality: Beyond the New Physics*.

The story of quantum physics is incomplete, so not all its explanations veto a materialist paradigm. Two of the theories, the hidden variables theory and the many universes theory, still hold onto old-school deterministic scientific interpretations, albeit with some farfetched assumptions required to make them feasible. But the dominant theory about quantum physics, the Copenhagen interpretation, says that on the atomic level, we alter reality by the act of observing it. In order to make sense of the physics with this twist in theory, we are faced with a proviso that consciousness itself creates physical reality.

And that, friends, is physics giving us its own version of a creation story.

Evidence of the psychic and paranormal through centuries appears to be begging humankind to acknowledge and study spiritual and paranormal dimensions, with potential applications for political, social, and environmental problems. Who knows? Psi may be the spiritual dimension itself at work. Schwartz says that "Spirit is not only willing and able to assist us but is insistent that we proceed" because it has "a broader understanding as to the urgency of the matter" than we do (Schwartz G. E., The Sacred Promise: How Science is Discovering Spirit's Collaboration with Us in Our Daily Lives, 2011, p. xxii).

If spirit can be tapped in ways beyond the seemingly "hit or miss" randomness of current experience, it could be employed to confront worldly issues. Philosophers sometime express a concern that technology has outpaced spiritual growth, with the evidence that an astounding 187 million people were killed because of human conflicts in the 20th century, representing one tenth of the world's 1913 population. (Braden, Choice Point 2012: The Promise of our Future in the Cycles of the Past, 2010, p. 3 (CD)) The time may be ripe for the spiritual aspect of science to help technology catch up, through a return to a dimension that has been lost. Society appears to be at a critical point in human evolution, given rapid technological change, overpopulation, air and water destruction, and even overwhelming evidence of sudden climate change and climate imbalance, all of which have impacts on whether Earth will remain a livable place. Perhaps the planet Venus is a harbinger, with its surface temperature between 800 and 900 degrees Fahrenheit. Given its distance from the sun, Venus' surface temperatures would be expected to be only 200 degrees, but scientists know that Venus experienced a runaway greenhouse effect, as we now know that carbon dioxide makes up 96 percent of Venus' atmosphere (Filippenko, 2007) How that happened is unknown, but this is a sobering consideration given the recent rapid increase of carbon dioxide in earth's atmosphere, but our awareness of this reality provides an opportunity to tackle it.

Research reported in 2009 by Nalini Ambady and Jamshed Bharucha at Tufts University indicated that the human brain literally reorganizes itself throughout life as it develops a cultural lens through which to perceive the world. That the human brain is partially formed in a cultural way is further evidence that today's materialistic paradigm about the makeup of our brains needs to be revisited. What if the approach to the paranormal was expanded from the western cultural lens of scientific experimentation to a broader viewpoint? Wahinkpe Topa suggested one possibility, which is to study reality with a mix of neuroscience and the indigenous wisdom of Native American cultures, whose wisdom about the natural world was collected over thousands of years under a very different perspective of reality (Topa, 2011, p. 3).

Clues about reality are hidden if our perspective is not wide enough to embrace them. Returning to the Gregg Braden's toaster example, we have no way to know if people were indeed able to use energy inherent in the cells of their bodies to toast bread without machines. Each human cell has 1.17 volts of electrical potential, and with 50 trillion cells in a human body, the amount of potential in the electromechanical field is enormous, without even touching the realm of the spiritual (Braden, Choice Point 2012: The Promise of our Future in the Cycles of the Past, 2010, p. 10 (CD)). The point of this tidbit of information is to say that open-minded scientific research would include human energy possibilities that exist "outside the box" and could uncover hidden abilities we fail to find because our beliefs are reluctant to accept the notion that such inherent abilities might exist. What if transportation devices and telephones were unnecessary because humankind had perfected long-distance transportation or communication without the assistance of external devices?

This is one of the potential applications of psi, once psychic abilities are well enough understood, and I am optimistic that "scientism" is giving way to the study of psi and consciousness survival. I hope that someone may read these words in 200 years and muse about how backward our thinking was and how many errors my speculation undoubtedly holds. This would show that the progress I would like to see will have been accomplished. And somehow, perhaps psychically, I believe that it will. The world of energy that we inhabit has more layers than science has yet isolated. And if we discover that science is the incorrect tool for studying spirituality, we will have learned to focus elsewhere. Secrets to some of humankind's most vexing problems could be "unfolding with assistance from the invisible elephant in the room known as Spirit" (Schwartz G. E., The Sacred Promise: How Science is Discovering Spirit's Collaboration with Us in Our Daily Lives, 2011, p. xv)

# 7

# THE BEST EVIDENCE—
# PERSONAL VALIDATION

UNREPORTED PSI EXPERIENCES PROVIDE NO benefit to society, but when we share experiences, the walls that imprison this potentially valuable resource will crumble. Anecdotal reports have convincing power, but in order to carry scientific validity, large numbers of such cases are necessary. But because having a paranormal experience is still considered "weird" by a large portion of the population, the ironic catch-22 is that such experiences remain weird because people fail to share them. The suppressed rate of reporting makes them seem rarer, and consequently weirder, than they are. But progress is happening. Those whose personal experiences convinced them of its reality supported privately funded organizations such as IONS, which has been conducting serious research on parapsychological phenomena using accepted research methods and uncovering dramatically significant evidence of psychic phenomena. Already, as the scientistic objection to the paranormal gradually erodes away, more people feel free to share their psychic experiences.

That said, one's own experiences, if treated honestly, are evidence of what is real or not. My own life experiences were the first and most convincing evidence I have for the value of psi. I trust my psychic and intuitive hits because I was clearly benefited when I followed them, while not following them often caused unnecessary suffering. Although I have had my share of seemingly pointless psychic urgings, the accuracy rate has been reliable enough to convince me of their authenticity. Although we have no proof and cannot explain what underlies the phenomenon, the abundant statistical evidence we have is solid. Although the magnitude of psi seems weak, that is likely because our lack of a solid understanding leaves us waffling about in a hit-or-miss way. Coupled with the evidence of my personal psychic experiences, some of which I will relay in the last part of this book, the levels of statistical significance for psi and the power of prayer are as close to proof as one can get. But the best proof is in the lived experience of people, where the value of real psi is being recognized and increasingly harnessed.

The late priest and healer, Ron Roth, relayed a story that he once got a clear intuitive foresight when he was a passenger in an automobile. On nearing a fork in the freeway, he got an unmistakable urge to take the less direct route (Roth, Divine Dialogue, 1999). He attempted to ignore this psychic hit because he was not driving. He would need to convince his friend to take a longer route. Shortly thereafter, their vehicle was bashed into by a multi-axle truck that slid into the side of their car. Ron was nearly killed in the crash, and he often remarked that he should have followed this clear-cut intuition.

As for validation of psi through personal experience, I particularly like the account of a Nebraska church that was destroyed in a 1950 explosion. It is illuminating because no one was killed or injured in the process, but given the circumstances, that fact was so unlikely that it begs for an explanation. At 7:27pm on March 1, 1950, a boiler in the church exploded and entirely destroyed the West Side Church in Beatrice, Nebraska (Mikkelson, 2013). No one was in the church at the time, although the choir had been scheduled to practice there at precisely 7:20pm that night. Typically attended by 15 members, every member of the choir, including the director, was either late or encountered something unusual that prevented him or her from attending on time that evening. When choir members were later interviewed, it was found that two members had car trouble, one was delayed by a vexing homework problem, one was "just plain lazy" about getting there on time, one fell asleep unexpectedly, one discovered that her dress was soiled, one wanted to hear the end of an interesting radio program, and there were other unusual reported reasons, such as simply not wanting to leave on time that night. It would be expected that for any given choir practice, some members typically attending would not be there or not be on time. But with a probability of one-in-four that any given member would not attend or be at least seven minutes late to practice, the odds that *every one* of 15 regular attendees was missing at the church seven minutes after the posted practice time is 1 in 1.1 billion, which means that the odds are prohibitively low that chance alone was operating. Yes, it *could* have been due to chance that no one was there that night, but these odds are much less likely than winning a Powerball jackpot with one ticket. Even a mindset attributing this to chance might encounter doubt against such long odds, indicating that something beyond simple chance was operating here.

Such circumstances are far more common than would be expected. Disasters *typically* have lower than average attendance. An intriguing pattern has appeared repeatedly in research, which is a tendency for some people to avoid unpredictable disasters. In this light, the Institute of Noetic Sciences' Dean Radin researched the history of jet aircraft crashes. He compared the number of people onboard aircraft that crashed with the number that would be normal for flights on the same day of the week and same time of the year. Consistently, the number of people onboard those unfortunate aircraft was considerably smaller than the number that typically flew on that day of the week. The results were highly significant, that in the aggregate, people possess some type of conscious or unconscious knowledge to avoid flights that will crash. Radin also showed that during the September 11th disasters in 2001, the first twin tower that collapsed in New York City held far fewer people when the doomed jet hit than was typical for that time and day of the week, again indicating some peoples' conscious or unconscious avoidance of the building that day. The second tower had far fewer people than average, but it was being evacuated after the first tower was hit, so this had an obvious reason. Still, the first tower's numbers echoed similar research on precognition at IONS, including a study reporting that a particularly large number of people had dreams of a tsunami in Asia shortly before a tsunami devastated parts of Indonesia in December 2004 (Radin D., Supernormal, 2013).

It is quite amazing that this factual and statistically validated research has received so little coverage. The mismatch between the actual and likely number of injuries or deaths in the church explosion, the Twin Towers on 9/11, and the relative paucity of people in airlines that crash receive little coverage because there remains the belief that these relationships must be due to coincidence. Essentially, the scientific materialist paradigm is ignoring statistical evidence that cannot be explained—since psychic intuition must be, after all, a fantasy of wishful believers! News stories typically note that "it was fortunate" that the number of potential victims on the day of a disaster was smaller than usual, but the prevailing view remains widespread that these anomalous mismatches are unrelated to some underlying explanatory phenomenon. It clearly is fortunate that the numbers are lower than expected, but the operative reason explaining why they were lower is a piece of information that should not be ignored. The seemingly fortuitous circumstance indicates that some people are consciously or unconsciously acting on intuitive hits to avoid pain, injury, or physical death. The possibility to teach whatever underlies this is a key to reduce future suffering.

What about those people who do board a jet that will crash? Why did they not get the message? People differ in their sensitivity and attention to such intuition, but a better understanding of intuition could have an abundant payoff. Although fewer people board doomed flights, many people do. Do these people have a death wish?

Probably not. More likely, the subtleness of psychic urges is the culprit. Even if a psychic message is obvious, the demands of our lives can be dogged, leading people to convince themselves that, despite misgivings, responding to intuitive tinges of fear would not allow them to go anywhere or get anything done. Time issues, business and family commitments, emotions, and the inconvenience and cost of changing an airline ticket mean that an intuitive hit not to board a particular aircraft better be blatant—as in "knock-me-down" obvious—before most of us will take action on it. Unfortunately, blatant messages are rarely the case. Often people surviving tragedies report that they had a suspicion to avoid the situation, but the inconvenience of changing their plans trumped this inkling of doubt. Most intuitive hits are more like whispers than shouts, easily overlooked in the business of our lives. It is also possible that, if it is your charted time to leave your earth existence behind, the wisdom of universal consciousness may not send you an intuitive hit at all.

Also, people with no belief in intuition at all will not interpret a psychic impression of any magnitude as anything more than an emotional thought. One of the most telling pieces of scientific research on psychic phenomena was reported in the 1940s by Gertrude Schmeidler, a president of the Parapsychological Association and a professor of psychology at the City University of New York. She published research showing that people who did not believe in ESP actually had little ESP. (Schmeidler, 1973). On the other hand, people who believed in ESP scored much higher on ESP tests. Apparently one's belief is a self-fulfilling prophecy, providing an example that

*You'll See It When You Believe It*, the clever title of Wayne Dyer's book describing the self-fulfilling consequences of belief.

That ESP would mostly show up in people who believe in it, even in a controlled laboratory study, is not surprising. People who receive and act on psychic events in their lives are obviously more likely to believe in the reality of ESP than people who do not experience it personally, or experience it so rarely as to attribute it to coincidence. Not only did Schmeidler's research demonstrate again the reality of ESP to a doubting society, but its results are curiously similar to the hard science research in quantum physics, which has confirmed that observation does indeed affect physical reality. And what is even more revealing is that research at the Institute of Noetic Sciences has shown that even clairvoyant observation causes a change in a quantum system. That is, a photon experiment conducted at a distance, with people "watching" it only in their minds, can still cause physical light to collapse into a particle. The impact is quite small, but it is fascinating that observing the phenomenon with one's eyes is not necessary. It can be observed in one's mind. This is truly challenging to fit into the materialist perspective of reality, but the evidence reveals that it is not only possible, but is happening (Radin D. P., 2013).

Undoubtedly, one of the biggest reasons that people doubt the existence of psi is precisely because psychic hits generally arrive in subtle ways that are hard to distinguish from imagination. Like a gentle breeze wafting around, it is difficult to grasp the message, and even if one is open to intuition, it may be difficult to decipher its meaning. Television and movie psychics are far more fortunate. These programs represent psychic messages as vibrant visual hits, but real intuitive messages for most of us are *much* more subtle. Clearly, we would prefer obvious psychic battering to a brush on the cheek by a psychic whisper that seems indifferent whether we act on it or not.

# 8

# IF IT'S REAL, WHY DON'T PSYCHICS WIN THE LOTTERY?

IT SEEMS LOGICAL TO ASSUME that practiced psychics should be good enough at following their psychic information to avoid their own personal pratfalls. But they mostly are no better at avoiding misfortunates than the rest of us. So why is that?

It is a legitimate question to ask. Like the rest of us, talented psychics regularly get into trouble they should have foreseen, and this undoubtedly contributes to the aggregate cynicism about psychic phenomena in our society. If they are so psychic, why do these people lose things like everyone else? And the really good question is "Why don't psychics regularly win lottery jackpots?" Of course, scientistic thinking says the obvious answer is that psychics are fakes (Hines, 2003). But in case you thought this question would put psychic mumbo jumbo to bed for good, let us look at the evidence.

# ■ The Problem of Magnitude: It's Real but Very Weak

. . . . . . . . . . . . . . . . . . . . . . . . . . . . . . . . . . . . . . . . . . . . . . .

There is more than one identifiable reason, but perhaps the main reason psychics do not disproportionately win the lottery is that the magnitude of psychic accuracy is small. That is not to say it does not exist. The evidence for the existence of psychic phenomena, as replicated in statistical meta-analysis, is overwhelming. Even though there remains a paucity of theory about what is going on, the studies have proven—as much as statistics can prove anything—that psychic phenomena exist. But I have noted that the psychic voice is often meek and, given our lack of understanding about using it, the error level is high.

The level of psychic ability varies from person to person, but the good news is that psychic abilities improve with practice. Dean Radin's experiments at the Institute of Noetic Sciences repeatedly show that people who practice meditation perform better in psychic tests, including those in which they are able to collapse the wave function in double slit photon experiments (Radin D., Entangled Minds, 2006). That is, meditators are better able than nonmeditators to change the wave and particle properties of light by simply imagining that they were observing the light. In other words, the peculiar property of quantum mechanics, whereby observation affects the properties of light, is more pronounced when done remotely among people who practice meditation. The reason appears to be an enhanced ability among meditators to remain steadfast in focusing on a task. This research again indicates that psi is real, but at least in the random way we employ it, psi has also been shown to be very weak. With the paucity of our current knowledge about strengthening it, we have a long way to go before we can harness these benefits to use our psychic abilities effectively.

Returning to the title of this chapter, picking lottery numbers psychically is not likely to get you a lottery jackpot. That is not because psi is not working, but because it is not working sufficiently. As a person who worked with estimating the finances of the Texas Lottery for many years, I have some knowledge and experience in calculating the odds of winning lottery jackpots. The evidence indicates that picking lottery numbers psychically may improve one's odds of picking correct lottery numbers by multiple times, but even if it is five times, the odds of winning lottery jackpots with psychic number picking are only slightly improved. Even if psychic picking of numbers without remuneration improves random odds by the hypothetical five times, the probability of winning a lottery jackpot in the multi-state Powerball lottery would improve from a miniscule 1 in 292 million to a still tiny 1 in about 58 million.

When probabilities of success are very low, such as winning a lottery jackpot with these odds, the laws of probability make it difficult to get enough trials to verify psychic accuracy. A study with one thousand, one hundred thousand, or even one million lottery picks would expect 0 jackpots using randomness and 0 jackpots with psychically-selected numbers. It would require about a billion trials to see obvious differences. Then we could expect about five random jackpots and about 26 psychically-selected jackpots. At one lottery pick of five numbers every 5 seconds for 16 hours a day, a billion picks would take more than 237 years. So, with what we know today, excellent psychics can improve their odds of winning a lottery jackpot substantially, but even an enormous improvement still leaves astronomically small odds of winning a jackpot. Whatever is going on in this realm of the psychic, the "noise" is overwhelming the parapsychological signal we want to isolate and understand.

Both Radin and McTaggart describe psychic tests that were highly significant in a statistical sense, but still not effectively applicable in the real world. In the aforementioned research with four pictures, if chance expects 25 out of 100 "correct" answers and a huge number of repeated trials finds an average of 32 correct answers, it is obvious that more than chance is going on. A statistical significance test showing that the odds of an event being due to chance is 1 in one trillion only tells us that something peculiar is happening, but it tells us nothing about the strength of the phenomenon and what underlies it. If we do not know how this seemingly magical information is acquired and the number of incorrect hits is large, we can hardly use it for anything useful. It remains in the domain of magic, which is fun in itself, but it fails to satisfy the part of us that wants to know how something works and how the phenomenon can be yoked for useful improvements in our lives.

Still, that psychic powers improve one's odds at picking lottery numbers is exciting, regardless of the magnitude of improvement. Critics of psi often cynically mention the "psi assumption", which states that any deviation from chance in psychic tests is assumed by believers that psychic phenomena are real. Their criticism argues that positive statistical results that occur are due to cheating researchers or quirky statistical trials, since the data show something that cannot be real. Detractors of the psi assumption begin with the belief that psychic phenomena are not real, having a predetermined mindset as guilty of bias as the side it attacks. They argue that, unless resulting from methodological flaws or fraud, highly statistically significant departures from chance should be categorized as simply "inexplicable to science" rather than be considered evidence of psi. Given the academic mindset claiming a bias in the psi assumption, Harvey Irwin argues that some scientists reject parapsychology simply because they "cannot accept its empirical findings" (Irwin, An Introduction to Parapsychology, 1989, p. 272).

If a psychic impression is too subtle to be recognized, it can easily be missed or misinterpreted. This may explain why statistical tests of psi include so many incorrect answers. If chance would expect 25 correct answers out of 100 trials and we repeatedly yield 32 correct answers, that is hugely significant statistically, but there were still 68 incorrect answers on the average. We are still getting more than two-thirds of the answers wrong, meaning that whatever this paranormal phenomenon is, it is not reliable or strong enough to be employed usefully. Although meta-analysis reveals overwhelmingly significant verification that psychic abilities are real, the small magnitude of psychic accuracy is an unfortunate reality.

## One of the Weirdest Results of Psychic Research

There is another reason why psychics are not winning lottery jackpots in identifiably greater numbers than the rest of us. In researching self-interested motives, Jose Silva, founder of the Silva Foundation, discovered that psychic intuition is more accurate when its purpose accomplishes some holistic or helpful purpose (The Silva Method, 2011). Self-serving and malicious motivations diminish and seriously erode the accuracy of psychic impressions, as though some guiding principle behind the energy insists that it be tapped for compassionate purposes only (Oschner, 1974). In light of the lottery question, an obvious problem with attempting to use psychic information to pick winning lottery numbers is having self-interested motives. On top of the magnitude issue already mentioned, psychic ability is eroded further when the motives of the psychic are selfish.

Without a life-enhancing holistic purpose, the Silva Foundation maintains that psychic accuracy plummets to levels only moderately above chance (Oschner, 1974). I recall what the late popular psychic Sylvia Browne said in this regard, as she relayed a colorful story about how she had often psychically located the lost purses of her female clients. Even so, if she lost her own purse, she said "it's gone". Professional psychics step in doo-doo as often as anyone. (Smolinski,

2010, p. 2). Apparently, the gift of psi is not intended to protect us from life's lessons, but it can assist us in helping others.

With this in mind, let's look at a wrinkle in the lottery example. What if one picks lottery numbers psychically for a charity, without any intention of keeping any of the winnings for oneself? Would this increase the psychic accuracy? The answer appears to be a cautious yes, but even here, the possibility of adulation for choosing the correct numbers gets the ego involved and appears to be enough self-interest to thwart the correct psychic picking of jackpot lottery numbers. Just the simple self-satisfaction of "knowing I did it" can doom the process. The small magnitude of psychic accuracy is made even smaller when self-interested motives are involved. The arena already is a loaded minefield in which psychic accuracy is far from 100 percent correct. Even if the apparent reality that psychic energy is diluted by self-interested motives is ignored, we need to know a great deal more about what psychic energy is before its level of accuracy can be enhanced and reliably employed.

## ■ What are the Odds Anyway?

· · · · · · · · · · · · · · · · · · · · · · · · · · · · · · · · · · · · · · · · · · · · · · · · · · ·

Doubters place emphasis on psychic errors rather than successes. Sylvia Browne was often criticized for failing to reach the 80 percent accuracy she occasionally claimed. Critics were fond of cataloguing her errors, but her accuracy level was still impressive enough to have amassed a huge following of fans. Admittedly, having a fan base is poor evidence of psychic ability, but something kept them as followers. Even fans will fade away if one's accuracy rate fails to exceed that of random luck.

Honest professional psychics acknowledge that they are often wrong, even on their best days. Determining the level of accuracy is difficult because laboratory settings are artificial and the number of errors is large, as noted by researchers at Princeton University and the Institute of Noetic Sciences (IONS). We have already seen that telepathic communication results in small improvements over chance, but on a more basic level, simply picking heads or tails psychically yields even less impressive results—51.2 percent correct, when chance alone is 50 percent (Radin D., The Conscious Universe: The Scientific Truth of Psychic Phenomena, 1997, p. 134). This small difference from randomness may look like a trivial difference, but with meta-analysis (the collective combination of huge numbers of studies with different participants, biases, and techniques), these percentage differences all but prove the reality of psi. Because the number of studies represented by the meta analyses over many decades is in the millions, the odds of getting 51.2 percent correct from chance alone is one billion to one (Radin D., The Conscious Universe: The Scientific Truth of Psychic Phenomena, 1997).

Research at the Institute of Noetic Sciences shows that our minds are capable of affecting random number generators, healing remotely, and even (amazingly) having success in retroactive prayer. That is, prayers can change the past as long as the person doing the praying does not know what already has happened, since knowledge of the past would "collapse the wave function" into a single reality. That ability was determined by interestingly designed studies of random numbers and prayer (Radin D. P., 2013). Studies of the efficacy of prayer have shown that time is not a factor for achieving positive results, and I like to think this is statistical validation for the indeterminacy of quantum physics, whereby something can exist in more than one state as long as it has not been observed.

Since prayer has been shown statistically to have positive effects retroactively, go ahead and pray for a particular outcome to an event you have video recorded but not yet watched! Research results indicate that you can pray while watching the recording, as though the action is unfolding at that moment. Perhaps it is silly to use prayer for something as petty as the outcome of a game, but consider this illustrative example. Can your prayer at that moment of watching the recording change the final score that has already been electronically reported and is printed in that unopened newspaper in your driveway? The answer is no, because that wave function has already collapsed. So what do the studies of retroactive prayer and psychic ability suggest? They indicate that as long as you do not know what the reported score was, your prayer after-the-fact can still affect what has already happened and what has already been reported. Your prayer can still have an impact on the past. That is kooky but it is consistent with experimental evidence that psychic influence is independent of time. Because of the limitations of experimentation, these studies showed only very small retroactive time effects, but they are nonetheless significant. Unfortunately, this intriguing clue about a relationship between psi and time itself is a topic far beyond the scope and possible limits of this book.

The research of Dean Radin, the Institute of Noetic Sciences, and the numerous studies described by Lynne McTaggart show that much progress has been made about the effects of our minds on mechanical devices and intentional outcomes, but because of a lack of theoretical knowledge and a limited prevailing worldview, the emphasis still remains on convincing people that the phenomena exist rather than on the pursuit of how they operate. Much of science is only now adjusting to Einstein's relativity, after centuries of entrenchment in Newtonian physics. Even quantum physics still has its doubters, regardless of the pervasive facts. Radin often mentions such roadblocks encountered in attempting to do his research. Particularly, he notes that the statistical significance levels that would be convincing in other areas of scientific research are considered inadequate when studying psychic and paranormal phenomena. If the odds are only 1 in 20 that an outcome is due to chance (the 0.05 level of significance), most social scientists will say that something real is responsible. For paranormal phenomena, that is not good enough.

CHAPTER

9

# BEYOND THE STATISTICS—
# HOW DOES PSI WORK?

INFORMATION RECEIVED PSYCHICALLY IS INFORMATION received by some other means than the five senses that Aristotle identified for getting information about the world. Psi includes fascinating yet controversial phenomena such as extrasensory perception (ESP), psychic healing, clairvoyance, intuition about the future (precognition), intuition about distant events, and mind over matter (psychokinesis).

We are at the stage of needing research into what is behind these phenomena. It helps us little to have overwhelming statistical evidence for the existence of psi, when the impact of subtle psychic messages for us is underwhelming, given the low magnitudes, frequent errors, and lack of knowledge on how to use psi. To increase the "how to" knowledge in the practical and spiritual realm, the focus should graduate to capturing what is going on.

One theory is that, on the most basic level, some psychic ability may be simply physical, grounded in hyperactive awareness that appears to exceed our five senses, but is actually grounded in them. It originates in sensory abilities that are subliminal, leaving us unaware that we have them. It is a misconception to believe that psi is always a form of extrasensory magic, even if it lies outside the realm of current scientific understanding. Nancy du Tertre is an attorney and successful psychic detective who argues in favor of this point. She says that most psi is grounded in intense awareness of sensory information, since we receive far more sensory input than we consciously realize. She attributes some of her "psychic" ability to training her brain not to ignore subtleties that are overlooked as the brain siphons through more information than we generally need (Du Tertre, 2012). Our senses know more than we are aware of knowing, rather like the subconscious mind residing outside our everyday awareness.

Intuitive hits in our daily lives do indeed have a rational component. When I get an intuitive feeling not to walk down a particular alley, this feels like simple common sense at work because I am aware of my surroundings and can draw from my past experience and training in similar circumstances. I can see what the buildings look like and I may react to how the area smells. I may even have pre-existing knowledge of past events in the area, and I can perceive sounds and the level of light. A sudden silence or shift in sounds provides me with information. I have layered rational knowledge and sensory input for the spirit to work with, so my psychic hit actually blends rational knowledge with the subconscious intuitive feeling. It can still be psychic, but it is not a message operating in a vacuum.

Some people claim to see auras, which may be a form of electroreception, which is the ability that sharks, eels, and rays use to perceive natural electric stimuli. This is an aptitude that may be limited to only some of us, and those that have it may not be aware of having it. People with this faculty may see auras but cannot explain why. The mysteries of why acupuncture and reiki work may also take root in bioelectricity. More evidence that our senses can gather information without our awareness has been discovered in the phenomenon known as blind sightedness. Notable cases include situations when a person's eyesight is fine, but there has been some damage to the brain's visual cortex, so visual signals getting to the brain are not processed properly. People with this condition can have an object placed in front of their eyes, but they do not perceive any object there. Yet they can identify notable characteristics of the object if they are asked about it, indicating that they are consciously aware of characteristics they cannot see. In a similar vein, our smell receptors actually detect the energy of vibrational quantum transitions in odor molecules, which was researched by G.M. Dyson in 1937. This means that some of our sense of smell may be grounded in infrared light that we cannot perceive with our sense of sight.

This says that psychic awareness of things not sensed may take root in physical circumstances, even if we are not consciously aware of them, meaning that some aspects of psi are partly drawn from known physical energies. This may be disappointing to that part of us that revels in wanting all psychic energy to drop magically into our awareness, but it is comforting to our pragmatic side that some of it already can be explained rationally.

Even so, this physical perspective of psi is distinctly not complete, since some psychic intuition exceeds the ability of our physical senses, such as the sensing of a current event happening thousands of miles away. If we get a precognitive dream about something that has not yet happened, this information could not have been acquired with our five senses alone, so we cannot loosely discard the part of psi that appears to be magic. If it is sensory information, it is sensory information obtained by more than our five commonly accepted senses, such as a physicality not yet understood. And certainly, consciousness surviving our physical deaths—an upcoming topic in this book—lies outside the realm of sensory input. History has repeatedly documented that mediumship and out-of-body experiences provide people with information that could not have been obtained by traditional means.

The concept of the Zero Point Field for universal communication has great potential, I think, for determining why we know things we should not, but this is a beginning theory. The zero point field is a quantum foam of virtual particles and photons. All types of elementary particles come into existence from nowhere and appear in our physical reality for a nanosecond before disappearing. These virtual particles are not stable enough to hang around, but blink in and out of existence. Lynne McTaggart, in her book entitled *The Field*, believes that this zero point field provides a common meeting ground for universal consciousness, as it could be tapped into by any conscious being to communicate and heal. Similarly, the universal oneness of consciousness at the heart of *A Course in Miracles* is a way in which psychic information might be universally available to everything. It is simply tapped into when needed.

Establishing a theory to research how paranormal phenomena work is a daunting task, and it cannot be tested until it is hypothesized. The testing state is a hurdle that must be overcome, but we cannot even see the hurdle yet. In the meantime, the paranormal will continue to be described with the "para" prefix, which in itself implies that it is beyond or beside reality rather than reality itself. The dominant scientific worldview still excludes the paranormal, so a testable theory is not being seriously pursued. The next step in understanding ourselves and our universe may come from researching what is currently outside the mainstream.

Psi evidently arises from some form of energy, but I have repeatedly remarked that science cannot link it to electromagnetic energy. Our grasp of electromagnetic energy allows engineers to construct buildings and spaceships and provides us with working smartphones. Quantum physicists say that about 70 percent of our universe is made up of what is called dark energy, the mysterious zero point energy that exists in a vacuum of space. Like psychic energy, this dark energy appears not to be electromagnetic, but it could be a medium that allows for the transference and sharing of psychic information. We are obviously in no position yet to research these esoteric and quantum realms, but at least they are a theory is progress, providing some stepping stones on how to proceed toward understanding and using psi. Once a theory becomes testable, research in the area will mushroom and parapsychology will take its place as a respected field of study.

## ■ Animal psi—it's not just for Human Animals

If psychic energy is real, it should be available to all conscious beings, and emerging research shows that animals also have innate intuitive abilities seemingly transcending those of their senses. In many cases, the innate abilities of nonhuman animals seem to transcend that of humans, perhaps because they do not question an intuitive inclination, as we are likely to do.

Because so many canines and cats share our lives, the most obvious examples of animal intuition are seen in them. Rupert Sheldrake noted that dogs know when their owners are coming home, so he researched this marvel and published a book outlining this ability (Sheldrake, 2011). In it, Sheldrake noted that canine pets display waiting behavior within a few minutes before their owners arrive home from trips. That would be expected if the owner arrives at the same time every day, but the canines in Sheldrake's experiments displayed enhanced expectation even when the arrival times of their owners were random and variable. Sheldrake's research has drawn its detractors, but most criticisms seem to arise from a disbelief of his premise more than his research methods.

My own dachshund, Daisy, repeatedly displays an example of intuitive ability that baffles me. Daisy has always disliked baths, yet I feel compelled to bathe her from time to time. I do not have a particular schedule for bathing my two dachshunds, and it varies widely from about two to six weeks. It simply occurs to me at some point that it has been a long time since I soaped them up. What is startling is that, on three separate occasions, Daisy knew when the *idea* came to me to give her a bath. Each time I was in a different room from her when it occurred to me that the doxies needed a bath, and a few seconds after the idea hit my mind, I noticed Daisy silently sneaking to her hiding place behind my bed, her tail down as though she was trying to escape something unpleasant. When this happened the first time, I remember wondering if this was an interesting coincidence. Maybe she had done something wrong at the time, but I never discovered anything unusual. But this uncanny behavior has happened more than once. When it happened again, I was intrigued. On the *third* time, it baffled me enough to deserve a mention here.

Being cynical that this could be a case of doxie clairvoyance, I have attempted to isolate what I might be doing to give Daisy hints, but Daisy's reaction preceded my doing anything but thinking. Perhaps this could take root in that supersensitive canine sense of smell. Could my thought give me a smell that she picks up? That seems unlikely but we know, for example, that canines can smell far more than we can. They possess, depending on the particular research report, at least 50 times the olfactory sensors as humans. Could this have been merely coincidence on three separate occasions? There is evidence that canine pets are extremely observant of the alpha dog in a pack or household, but if that is the case, she has picked up some extremely subtle hints I am not aware of providing. That also seemed highly unlikely since I was in a different room from Daisy when the thoughts came to give her a bath. Given that I am now convinced that psychic phenomena are real, I think it is far more likely that my lovable little pooch is displaying animal psi. Once again, the evidence is anecdotal but it points toward the reality of a phenomenon that we do not understand. Without wanting to overstate what is happening here, this fits within the theory that psychic information could be drawn from a field of universal consciousness.

As with the canine sense of smell, other animal senses are often remarkably more enhanced than our own, so what appears to be a paranormal psychic awareness in animals may be rooted in regular sensory experience, such as Nancy de Tertre's theory of subliminal hypersensitivity. Bats can sense their location by reverberating echoes, due to their remarkable hearing. There is anecdotal evidence that animals sense the vibrations of impending earthquakes, and although difficult to study, sensory input can evolve and be enhanced with time and usage. Oscar, a Rhode Island cat, attained media attention for accurately predicting the deaths of 25 nursing home residents over a 25 year period, but his particular abilities were not common to other cats (Dosa, 2011). What remains unknown is whether he was somehow psychic or just had a particularly refined sense of smell in comparison to other felines.

Some animals display sensitivity to magnetic fields. German and Czech researchers, in a two year study, determined that dogs spontaneously align their bodies with the earth's magnetic fields when they defecate (Vlastimil Hart, 2013). This may be a peculiar subject for study, but it seems relevant to the uncanny ability of dogs and cats to make their way home when they find themselves many miles away. Dogs, cats, deer, and foxes seemingly pick up information from magnetic fields, a quality known as magneto reception, and perhaps in some vestigial way, humans may have this dormant ability too.

To summarize, what appears to be psychic in humans and other animals may be rooted in our ordinary senses, although we are not aware of it. When we get a hunch about something without an obvious reason, the cause may be that our senses have picked up faint information, perhaps from a vestigial ability some animals have and that humans have mostly let atrophy over time. Yes, some of what we call psychic may arise because our senses are subliminally responsive to electromagnetic influences that are simply too subtle for our conscious awareness but still perceptible by our body and mind. Without denying the more supernatural nature of some psi, hyperawareness is at the root of certain abilities that appear psychic even to the person getting the information.

# 10

# QUANTUM PHYSICS HINTS AT THE REALITY OF PSI

WHAT WE ARE WITNESSING TODAY is a quiet whisper of change with profound implications. Nature itself is breaking the old rules of scientism and materialism in quantum physics, and one need not be a priest of physics to perceive and be affected by this. It might help to be a physicist to grasp the underpinnings of quantum physics, but whether we understand it or not, nature will have her way. The fun part for those of us interested in the paranormal is that reality is increasingly proving to be more than the old paradigm most of us were taught and believe, and it is far more interesting than our typical daily experience reveals.

To appreciate how utterly fascinating the implications are, a touch of quantum physics for those unacquainted with it will be useful here. I do not pretend to have the knowledge and experience to derive the mathematical conclusions, but that is not necessary for providing an overview. Understanding the math is not necessary to share in the more fascinating implications that theoretical research has revealed.

GARY G. PREUSS, PH.D.

The old classical belief accepted by scientists with more fervor than one could find in church pews was that what we observe "out there" in the world and universe is independent of us. It was held firmly that things out there exist whether we are here or not. This is the physical theory of realism, and it simply says that reality exists whether it is observed or not, that a tree falling in the forest makes sound waves whether anyone is there to perceive it. This seems very reasonable and fits within a perceptual sense of reality. Our perceptions are designed for survival in a macroscopic world, but the underlying microscopic reality remains hidden from them. That observation can affect reality is obvious in a macro sense, as observing your Aunt Stella in the bathroom will have an effect if she knows you are observing her (!), but it comes as a surprise to our practical side that even light itself is affected by being observed. Incredibly, light acts as a wave when it is not observed, but as soon as one observes it (or attaches a measuring device to observe it), light acts as a particle. A layperson's explanation of this can be seen in an entertaining video entitle "Quantum Physics Debunks Materialism", which I hope will still be available when you read this at https://www.youtube.com/watch?v=4C5pq7W5yRM. This is just one of the scientific facts that speaks of a universe far more conscious than we realize, and this reality opens doors that may explain psychic phenomena and ongoing consciousness beyond our physical bodies.

Another peculiarity of quantum physics is the aforementioned concept of nonlocality, also known as action at a distance. It turns out that individual atoms may be entangled, whereby an entangled atom in one part of the universe can (and does) have an immediate effect on its partner in another part of the universe, without any transmission medium between the two. Hence, the word nonlocality, since entangled atoms need not be close to each other for one to have an immediate effect on the other. Albert Einstein initially dismissed this spooky action and had a series of debates with Neils Bohr about it, but experimentation has now shown that one entangled atom does affect its partner in another part of the universe and the effect is instantaneous, not requiring a transmission medium and not being constrained by the speed of light. That is what troubled Einstein, since his law of special relativity said that nothing can be transmitted faster than the speed of light. Yet our macroscopic logic makes it seem necessary that some type of message must to be transmitted between the separate particles for one to affect the other. Instantaneous interaction between two particles separated by large distances seems foreign to our "real world" perceptions. These quirky implications look like fantastic philosophy dreamed up by a science fiction author, yet the solid evidence for nonlocality was the result of experimentation and mathematical calculations, such as exhaustive tests of John Stewart Bell's hypothesis known as Bell's Theorem. In our search for a theoretical basis for psi, entanglement could very well explain telepathy, which shares the nonlocality properties of being instantaneous and unaffected by distance.

What implications these subatomic realties have at the much larger level of our physical bodies is a subject under substantial discussion and experimentation today. We know from experimental quantum mechanics that matter does not even exist until it is observed. This is indeed spooky, but the research continues to find the same conclusions. What science must relegate to calling empty space may actually be a field of intelligent energy that has the power to arrange itself in productive ways. This also could be the source of some psi, intuitive knowledge, healing, and the means by which prayer works. We have discussed the positive statistical relationship between prayer and healing, but how God or universal intelligence carries out spiritual healing would be useful to understand, opening an exciting amalgam of possibilities.

We have grown to trust our perceptions in order to keep our bodies alive. If we cannot see it, hear it, touch it, taste it, or feel it, we are tempted to decide that it does not exist, or if it does, it is irrelevant. Mostly this serves us well for survival, but our limited perceptions can delude us. What looks like reality to us is a shadow of reality, well exemplified by the English physicist and philosopher, Sir James Jeans, who expanded on Plato's allegory of the cave (Jeans, 1931). In it, people are chained in a cave in such a way that they can only see a cave wall in front of them. Yet there is a room behind their backs, and there is a fire in the room, so things passing behind them but in front of the fire make shadows on the cave wall they see in front of them. Their entire view of reality is composed of these shadows that are cast, and this allegory represents how we perceive reality. As much as 90 percent of our universe is comprised of dark energy and dark matter, which our perceptions cannot perceive at all. Because of the intense gravity of black holes, from which even light itself cannot escape, black holes are invisible, hence "black". Even where light is available, most of the light spectrum that exists is invisible to our eyes, and since our perceptions can perceive only finite bits of reality, we only see a tiny part of the entire continuum.

From this small perspective, classical physics is a more comfortable perspective than the hokey world of quantum physics, which does not appear to match up with day-to-day experience and has unbelievable implications. If physics were not proving otherwise, our senses would insist that matter is something solid, although this apparent solidness is due to the stable quantum states of electron orbits that are mostly filled. But it is still energy gaining its apparent solidity from something akin to those rapidly moving fan blades. Solid matter is almost entirely empty space subject to a dizzying array of tendencies and probabilities, blinking in and out of existence.

So, what does this have to do with psi? According to the writings of Richard Cohn Henry and Stephen R. Palmquist, the reason materialists insist on a physical reality independent of the mind is that reality created by our minds would mean that consciousness, and not the physical world, is the ultimate reality. Henry and Palmquist argue that following these recent scientific experiments to a logical end would conclude that theism is the most rational explanation for consciousness, or at least that it is more rational than materialism (Russell, 2002). Peter Russell is a physicist and psychologist who points out that the existence of consciousness is undeniable, although it remains scientifically inexplicable. Through a process of research and scientifically-based logical reasoning, he came to the conclusion that consciousness is the ultimate reality, taking the road of logical reasoning to move from scientific agnosticism to faith. He believes that physics itself simply describes consciousness, writing that "space and time are not...fundamental dimensions of the underlying reality. They are fundamental dimensions of consciousness (Russell, 2002, p. 56).

Other researchers have arrived at this same conclusion in different ways. John Von Neumann and Eugene Wigner, in critiquing the various interpretations of quantum physics, attempted to make sense of its strangeness without desperately clinging to deterministic assumptions such as an infinity of universes. Not surprisingly, one peculiarity that von Neumann and Wigner could not explain was how electrical signals in the brain could become consciousness. Nonetheless, von Neumann said that the collapse of the wave function—whereby a photon decides to be a wave or particle based on whether it is observed or not—could not be a physical process. That means that something outside of physics would need to intervene. He rather reluctantly decided that consciousness was the only reasonable explanation. Wigner, who won a Nobel Prize in physics, concluded in his "Remarks on the Mind-Body Problem" (Wigner, 1983) that "it is not possible to formulate the laws of quantum mechanics in a fully consistent way without reference to consciousness."

Even if we accept the hypothesis that consciousness exists independently of our bodies, the creation and molding of matter by consciousness brings up another dilemma. If consciousness is primary and creates reality, then there can only be one consciousness in our universe. If there more than one consciousness, I would create one reality with my consciousness and you would create a different reality with yours. While each sentient being may perceptually have an individual consciousness, a unified reality would require a single unified consciousness. To solve this dilemma, it could be argued that all seemingly individual consciousnesses are pieces of one whole, rather like various radio frequencies sharing the same airwaves, but it is the totality of all consciousness that produces reality. With this requirement, physics sounds like religion telling us that God is in all things, at least all consciousness. According to Johanan Raatz, a physicist blogger and author, the obvious inference is that science has not buried God but revealed God, and in the process, buried materialism (Raatz, 2013).

At the risk of oversimplifying for the sake of clarity, what remains in our crucible is that mysticism and theism may indeed be the reality that best fits this new paradigm. In stark contrast to the science of the past, where it was believed that matter could be distilled down to finer and finer particles that could ultimately be discovered to reveal their mechanistic structure, pioneering physicists often become mystics today, although this mysticism is not mystical but grounded in experimentation and logic. They are aware that classical physics works within a very limited chunk of all reality (Jauregui, 2007, p. 32), while quantum physics is bringing us to the logical conclusion that conscious observation creates reality. Physicist Nick Herbert likened this to King Midas, who found himself robbed of the experience of life because everything he touched turned to gold. Herbert notes that our experience of reality is always compromised because everything that we observe turns to matter (Quantum Reality, 1985, p. 194).

The Jesuit physicist, priest, and visionary, Teilhard de Chardin, posited this in the mid-20th century, when he concluded that physics and spirit were both necessary to be complete. The relativistic and quantum physicist Olivier Costa de Beauregard's interpretation is that quantum physics, rather than shying away from psi on the basis of classical notions, "demands" that psi phenomena exist (Olivier Costa de Beauregard (1911-2007)).

It is odd that science is unfolding in a way that is reminiscent of its origins. The concept of "aether" serving as a universal medium through which light could travel was discarded as hokum, and now the concept of consciousness acting as a universal medium is embraced by a growing number of scientists. Consciousness is a far cry from aether, but the universal implications and consequences are the same. We noted that Isaac Newton was quite a spiritual man who felt pressured to remove descriptions of spirit in publishing his classical physics. His pared-down scientific cosmology had three centuries of entrenchment before slowly getting replaced by something closer to his original formulation. It took nearly the entire 20th century for the new paradigm to gradual erode away materialistic and "scientistic" ways of thinking, and this process remains far from complete in our societal thinking today.

Psi, as evidenced by its name, ought to be categorized in the realm of psychology, a branch of the social sciences, yet the social sciences lag behind the physical sciences in this transition. Given the recent advances of physics taking root in experimentation and quantum theory, the physical sciences are embracing a more welcoming attitude toward psi than the social sciences, which remain more wedded to traditional materialism. Survey research has shown that physicists are more likely to believe in the reality of psi than social scientists (Du Tertre, 2012). This may be surprising, but the physical sciences have not embraced psi so much as they are being led to it by new findings and research. Social scientists have yearned to have the rigorous respect of the "hard" sciences; so, when you are seeking something as firm as Planck's constant, you are not inclined to accept something as quirky as psi.

The apparent existence of a universal consciousness has fantastic implications not only for psi but for individual consciousness survival. It remains a dilemma how science can even study consciousness.

Still, there is no initial cause that allows the brain, which is matter and which we know is equivalent to energy itself, to generate consciousness. And if there is only one universal consciousness, the part of it that we somehow share does not have an independent existence for each of us. It is only borrowed while we are in our bodies, and when we die physically, the part of us that is conscious is not bothered by the apparent transition to a previous state. It may simply jump back into the universal pool of consciousness.

I realize this sounds weird, and perhaps I am getting duped by the implications. I bring this up now because I realize that evidence is not proof. Still, evidence is as close as we will get to proof while living in bodies. This is particularly true for consciousness survival after physical death, which I turn to now. So buckle in for the next leg of our journey, as we unravel what science has uncovered as evidence for consciousness survival.

# PART III

## THE SURVIVAL OF CONSCIOUSNESS

CHAPTER

11

# WHISPERS OF
# CONSCIOUSNESS SURVIVAL

MANY TIMES I HAVE WITNESSED the psychic medium, John Holland, relaying information from a discarnate person who has passed on. In his practice of mediumship, John ramps up his energy and shares messages from the "Other Side" to friends and relatives of their departed love ones. I have witnessed some astounding accuracy in his readings and have listened to him describe this process of mediumship in conversation and lectures. When he delivers messages from the Other Side in front of an audience, he says that the discarnate beings will "line up" to give messages to their loved ones in the audience. He admits to having no control about who comes through, as he is only the mediator who is aware and practiced enough to receive and transmit energy-based messages.

On one occasion, I was seated directly in front of a woman who happened to have a deceased spouse who was giving John a message for her. John first identified that the message was for someone in the area where I was seated, and after several of his statements, this woman began to cry. I had already talked to her socially before this event, and afterwards I turned around to ask her again about her emotion. She said that she was shocked to be chosen and was astounded that the personal information John had provided about her loved one was not only correct, but it included something that only she and her beloved spouse had ever shared. She was astonished when John mentioned this. Doubters often point out that information is widely available to mediums like John, but this particular snippet of personal information was not something John could have researched or found on the Internet.

We have seen that there is solid statistical substantiation for the existence of psi, but is there equivalent evidence extending to the survival of consciousness after our bodies die? This is a belief that most faith traditions hold, but conventional science has generally shied away from addressing the issue. The scientific tools to do so are not available, so if you thought studying psi scientifically was difficult, this task of studying consciousness survival is unquestionably even more challenging. But it is possible to study mediumship scientifically, which the Windbridge Institute in Tucson, Arizona, has been doing since 2008 (www.windbridge.org). The accuracy level of reputable mediumship indicates that mediums are not simply "making up" what they are reporting. When they relay information that is not known by anyone at the time—but later verified—this precludes simple cheating. A big question is whether mediums such as John Holland, John Edward, Gordon Smith and those involved in research at the Windbridge Institute are really communicating with the spirit of someone who has died. Just because mediums receive messages that can be verified as accurate does not necessarily mean that the medium is communicating with a person who has died. It is possible that mediums are simply superpsychic. Rather than communicating directly with a discarnate spirit, they may be getting information psychically from acquaintances of the departed person or from energy fields left behind when a person dies.

So, what evidence is there to distinguish whether mediums are communicating with the physically dead, getting psychic messages from living associates, or picking up some other energy? Let's look at some theories. The energy field theory of psychic mediumship is that the consciousness of each of us is a form of energy that remains on earth when our bodies die. Physics tells us that energy, at least electromechanical energy, cannot simply disappear, but gets transformed from one form to another. This is the energy that may hang around on earth, giving rise to hauntings and other spookiness. Under this theory, a medium attempting to communicate with the dead is simply picking up this energy field left behind when the person died, rather than actually communicating with the discarnate person.

But this is just one of theories. Another says that the medium is getting psychic information from people still living in physical bodies, or telepathy. Neither of these is proven, and neither excludes the circumstance of the person still being conscious on the Other Side. On the contrary, the predominant evidence leans in the direction that the medium is making actual communication with a departed spirit, to the degree that all mediums I have encountered insist that they *know*, rather than believe, that we consciously live on after our bodies die.

Once again, there are inauthentic charlatans claiming to be mediums, so we need to sift out the counterfeits. Fraudulent mediums could cheat by researching life stories in advance of a mediumship reading. Fortunately, true mediumship usually involves unheralded events in the lives of ordinary people, as with the emotional woman I spoke to about the message from her deceased husband. In public mediumship readings, it is rather convincing in itself when some reluctant audience member recognizes the information in a reading and reveals obvious emotional surprise that the medium not only narrowed down who the message was for but mentioned a secret only known to that person and his or her deceased loved one. I know personally that many people in John Holland's audiences were skeptics who admitted to simply accompanying a spouse or friend who really wanted to attend. It is particularly moving and convincing when discarnate spirits "drop in" to carry a message to these surprised and reluctant tag-alongs.

Occasionally, a message comes from someone who died long before anyone in the session or audience was alive. I find the best evidence for true mediumship is when very detailed information is revealed, but no one recognizes it, only to have the intended recipients of the message discover the truth of its meaning later. Some of these people who do not recognize the information will deny it at the time, but more commonly, people are taken aback by the accuracy of obscure hits. Often, those who denied the truth of a mediumship statement during a public or private reading later discovered that it was true.

I was in the audience in a public mediumship reading at a Hay House event in Atlanta many years ago when one such event happened (Holland, "I Can Do it", 2002). The medium was several minutes into the program, attempting to speak about the fundamentals of mediumship. He suddenly stopped and said that an image was pestering him. He was being hounded by a spirit to report that someone in the audience was affected by an apartment collapse happening at that moment in Chicago. He was mentally seeing floors of an apartment building collapsing. Mind you, this was during the days when cellular telephones were handheld devices with antennas, and the only electronic device this medium had was a microphone. The next day it was reported in the newspaper that an apartment building had collapsed in Chicago, and I was amazed that the event had happened at the exact time the medium sensed the floors collapsing. We also found out the next day that someone in the audience had a relative who lived in the collapsed building. The doubter in me looks for holes in stories like this, so I try to contact the people affected. A medium is not going to arrange an apartment collapse a thousand miles away to convince his audience that his mediumship is real. When I find no reasonable cause to doubt such events, I consider this type of anecdotal event to be quite convincing evidence.

Again, I realize that anecdotal stories are not airtight scientific evidence, but these stories, provided they are authentic, still reveal that something inexplicable to our senses is going on. During a cruise ship presentation by Sonia Choquette and John Holland in 2014, I was seated next to a recent friend who had honed her psychic skills and used them professionally. And although I am far from a professional psychic, my meditation practice and lifetime of prayer has given me some intuitive abilities that still surprise me. I also was blessed to have experienced 30 days of silence as a Jesuit novice, benefiting greatly from the contemplative lessons learned in the Spiritual Exercises of St. Ignatius. So, when John and Sonia were interacting with someone in the audience, I intuitively picked up a specific message. Just as I received it, my friend next to me remarked that she also picked up the same intuitive message! Even after many years of such remarkable events, such events still enliven the peculiar feeling I got in the first Silva course I took, which is "Where did that come from, and more importantly, how did I get the identical message my friend was getting?" But that was not all. John and Sonia onstage then announced they "got" the same message my friend and I had intuited. Welcome to the world where the bizarre is normal.

I found this exciting and intriguing, probably because the doubter in me still exists, and I love improbable verifications of psychic and spiritual hits. The repetition of such unlikely events has long since convinced me of the reality of psi, although it still does not answer whether the source of the message is telepathy with other people in the audience, an energy field, or communication with a discarnate person. What I know for certain is that I psychically got the same stated message as three other people and I was not cheating.

Such hints that verify psychic and mediumship messages are really quite common if we remain aware and mindful of them. Years ago at a presentation in Las Vegas, I experienced an episode of mediumship at, coincidentally, another John Holland seminar (Holland, 2008). I was one of three people called to the stage to enter a meditative state. I spent most of the session in meditation while other "cases" were done, and I was the last one left on stage. I kept getting visions of a woman named Agatha, finely dressed in attire appropriate to upper class British women around 1900. It reminded me of a scene from the 1964 movie, *My Fair Lady*, set at the Royal Enclosure of the Ascot horse race. Agatha had a message for a particular woman in the audience. When I was asked what visions I was getting, they matched up with the grandmother of someone in the audience, and very interestingly to me, the information that John was telling this woman was the same information I had received during my time in meditation. This was not general information, but a name and dress that were quite unusual to a particular point in time. I did not feel I was engaging in a conversation with anyone discarnate, but I was getting clear visual images and found it intriguing that these images were consistent with John's, including the name of the woman, which John picked up as either Agnes or Agatha, which the woman in the audience verified to be correct.

Can science tell us the source of these messages? Are we hearing from people who have passed on, giving us evidence for consciousness survival? While the study of psi can be operationalized into research amenable to a laboratory experiment, consciousness survival is an entirely more complex endeavor. Still, there is more than faith telling us that our consciousness survives after death.

CHAPTER

# 12

# CONSCIOUSNESS...NOW
# AND AFTER WE DIE

SCIENCE CANNOT TACKLE THE QUESTION of consciousness survival because it must initially get to first base, which is understanding consciousness itself, and this remains undone. If we do not understand what we are studying, there is no foundation to study whether it disappears at death, is transformed, or merely continues as it was after death. Perhaps the reason that a unified theory remains elusive to science is because consciousness itself is well beyond the limits of our contemporary scientific tools. Even so, the focus of this chapter is to look at the scientific evidence such as it is.

The question of whether our consciousness dies or moves on has intrigued people throughout history, so first I acknowledge my uneasiness with injecting this topic as though I have stumbled across some new revelation. This is terrain that has been vastly discussed and argued about throughout human history, but in my defense, the exploration of hardcore evidence is a rare endeavor that is nowhere near complete. I suspect that religious traditions are on target when they tell us that we live on after death, and I have faith in that regard, but relying on faith is frustrating to anyone with an empirical inclination that wants evidence.

Materialism maintains that our brains produce consciousness, and if that is so, it seems quite obvious that our consciousness will die with our bodies. But it may come as a surprise that hard evidence that our brains somehow produce consciousness is quite shallow. The "evidence" that our brains produce consciousness is grounded in the simple materialist perception that it looks that way. It looks that way because we see that when living creatures die, their consciousness drops out of view and seems to disappear completely. To our admittedly unreliable perceptions, a dead body looks like nothing more than a blob of organic matter that once had a living spirit inhabiting it. More so, our perceptions tell us that, while we live in our bodies, our consciousness goes where our brains go. Rarely is one's consciousness disconnected from one's body.

It also "looks that way" because science has found one-to-one correspondences between stimulating a part of the brain and eliciting particular physical or mental responses. Experiments have correlated what parts of the brain relate to vision, movements, muscular activity, autonomic functions of our hearts and other organs, and even mental processing and decision-making. Nonetheless, science is utterly mystified in locating an instigator of the decision-making process—that invisible driver that *decides* to move my legs so I can walk or run, which is consciousness itself.

Correlation is not causality, so the physical part of the brain that is stimulated before I move my fingers is not automatically the source of my conscious decision to move my finger. We can see electrical activity that correlates with thoughts, but we have no idea how or where the thought to move one's finger arises, and science cannot even locate the origin of a thought in the brain. At least for now, the driver of thought, or consciousness, is well outside our knowledge of brain chemistry and physiology.

Science is not reluctant to study consciousness because it wants to ignore it, but the scientific method simply cannot "go there". Although doctoral programs address the study of consciousness, science cannot explain its origins or even how it functions, but it clearly has played a major role in spiritual traditions. While the materialist mindset has held for a couple of centuries that consciousness arises in the brain and dies with the brain, most faith traditions insist that we continue to live consciously in an afterlife or in reincarnations.

This is a profound reason for the long-persisting dichotomy between scientism and religion. Inspirational teachers and even T-shirts (!) tell us that we are spiritual beings having a bodily experience. Spiritual traditions point to lives other than this one, many even indicating that we will be punished or rewarded depending on how we live our earthly lives. The Christian tradition may have put a seemingly excessive emphasis on a bodily resurrection, but it recognizes that some type of consciousness (or soul) exists after the body dies. It would make no sense for Christians to pray that the dead intercede for us, if those who have died are unconscious until they reconnect with the body at some point in the future. As such, even the Christian tradition accepts that a body is not necessary for consciousness to exist.

One obvious fact we do know about consciousness is that it exists, but that, unfortunately, is about all that can be said with certainty. It appears to be some type of energy, but like psi, an energy that remains elusive. The scientific theories that comprise our current understanding of the universe are grounded in electromagnetism, but consciousness—if it is indeed a form of energy at all—has none of the hallmark characteristics of electromagnetic energy.

Although consciousness cannot be neatly encapsulated and science has been compelled to ignore it, it may very well be the missing link in explaining the world of psychic phenomena and healing. Psi and consciousness survival share the same turf. Consciousness would be the centerpiece of life outside the body after physical death, unshackled by the space and time limitations of the body.

Multiple personality disorder presents a bit of evidence that consciousness and the body are not the same. In multiple personality disorder, one body has more than one personality, and the personalities essentially "time share" the body. How the personalities arise and the distinctions between them are not clear to science. Generally, each personality is unaware of the other(s) occupying the same body at different times, and only becomes aware of the others by the behavioral consequences of the other personalities. The distinction between personalities can be so pronounced that different personalities have been found to have different eyeglass prescriptions, which seems physically impossible. Try explaining that from a purely physical interpretation of consciousness. The existence of more than one consciousness in the same body indicates that different personalities can connect and disconnect with the body at will. The simplest explanation of this oddity is that the body is not the source of consciousness. As such, the body is unnecessary for the survival of personality and the death of the body is irrelevant to the existence of consciousness. This is just one indication that consciousness survives death, so stay with me.

Regarding the evidence for life after death, I waffle between my faith side and the "show me" side that yearns for proof. My intuition supports my faith that a designer gave us consciousness, and it seems irrational that we would be given consciousness for just a short lifespan on earth. What would be the point of life's often difficult lessons if what we learn will simply disappear when we die? If we are conscious for only the duration of our earthly lives, it would be rather pointless to spend our lives learning and experiencing.

Out-of-body experiences do indicate that our consciousness can exist somewhere that our brain is not, with implications for consciousness after the brain and body die. I have little personal experience with consciousness outside my body. The one time I began having an out-of-body experience, feeling all the vibrations of consciousness moving outside my body, my dachshund sensed something unusual and quickly walked over to place her head on my thigh, causing the imminent escape of my consciousness from my body to collapse back. Outside that event, my closest experience with consciousness leaving my body happened during the 30-day silent retreat with the Jesuits in November, 1985. At that time, I was walking through the Los Padres National Forest in the mountains north of Montecito, California, deep in meditative contemplation. My next memory was clinging to the side of a mountain, holding onto rock outcroppings and wondering how I got there (and of course, wondering how to get my body down from there!) I consciously planned how to get down step by step, but I have no memory of how I got my body into that precarious place. My consciousness for once had not been directly connected with my body at the time.

Another quirky touch of evidence for consciousness survival at death is that people's bodies lose a bit of mass immediately after dying, even when accounting for air loss in the lungs. Dr. Duncan MacDougall found a slight loss of weight at death but this would only be meaningful evidence of soul departure if consciousness or spirit had mass itself (MacDougall, 2010). If not, the result is probably due to the poor quality of the scales available at the time (1901) or even evaporating perspiration at the point of death. More intriguingly, some people have perceived what appear to be living entities leaving the bodies of people who are dying. But I have already noted the danger of relying on perception as evidence. The stories are nonetheless noteworthy, and the devil's advocate might say that perception can be right as well as wrong.

Perceptions need variability to understand something, and like the existence of oxygen in our atmosphere, things that do not vary much are difficult to perceive at all. For example, the only reason we have a tactile sense of temperature is because it varies. If we lived in a universe where temperature was always constant, we would have no concept of temperature at all. Likewise, if God was suddenly a little less or a little more present, then God would be blatantly obvious to our perceptions, but a God who is constantly omnipresent—always here and not varying—is exactly why God seems distant. We do not perceive the existence of an omnipresent God because of God's constancy, since the unvarying constancy means our perceptions have no variability to work with. I bring up these examples to point out that when we witness the death of a brain, the appearance that consciousness has disappeared may be just one more deceptive perception. Because of our perceptual limitations, the apparent destruction of consciousness at death can easily be an illusion.

Since our perceptions can be duped, gathering evidence on consciousness survival is very tricky. There is no question that our bodies die, and our perceptions have nailed that one. But our consciousness or spirit is the true essence of our being and the jury remains out as to whether consciousness continues after we die. Gregg Braden argues that the physics of the very small world and the very large realms have become disconnected, but "the missing link in the unified physics falls under the umbrella that we think of as *consciousness*." (Braden, 2008, p. 172)

## ◼ Taking Sides: Why we do NOT believe our consciousness survives death

What causes us to doubt that our consciousness survives death? It is back to perception. If left to the evidence we perceive with our senses, the most apparent conclusion of our perceptions is that we do not survive death. Our earthly experiences tell us every day that we are our bodies. We perceive that our consciousness goes where our bodies go, and only in exceptional circumstances do we find our bodies and consciousness not glued together. If my eyes and brain are in my bedroom, my awareness at that moment is in my bedroom, and in the sporadic cases when it is not, this is viewed as a dream or an unreal aberration. If my body is in Europe, my consciousness perceives Europe around me. Only rarely are we fortunate enough to have out-of-body experiences where we witness things happening in places away from our bodies. Many of us live our entire earthly lives without having even one such experience. So most of us live in a world where our bodies and spirits seem indistinguishable. Evidence of this perception is obvious in the news media, when reporters often report that the victim of a drowning was found in 10 feet of water, rather than reporting that it was the *body* of the victim that was found. If consciousness survives death, the dead body of Joe Smith is no longer the essence of Joe Smith, but the common perception appears to be that it is.

The Doubting Thomas in me comes back to how closely our consciousness seems glued to our bodies. Even the effects of drugs and injuries on our consciousness seem to point to a consciousness that depends on the brain for existence. It is not rocket science to see that our consciousness is affected and even shut down by drugs affecting one's brain and nervous system. This correspondence looks so solid that suppressing our brain with a drug that inhibits neuronal activity, such as sodium pentothal or propofol, knocks out our consciousness. Likewise, Alzheimer's disease and brain injuries seem to indicate that consciousness is dependent on the brain. People with Alzheimer's disease do not appear to be consciously present, so it appears that brain degradation is responsible for the loss. And what about all those correlations between stimulating parts of the brains and certain transcendental emotional states and behaviors? So it does look at times that our brain is the driver, even if the inability to isolate such a driver may be due to immature science. If consciousness can survive without the brain, why is it that brain damage has such a profound effect on our consciousness? We will explore this soon, but for now, these correlations are reasons we are tempted to believe that consciousness is generated by the brain and reasons not to believe in consciousness survival.

Also, when people die, communication with them appears to end. There are no more telephone calls, no more text messages, and no more conversation with them. If they loved us on earth, it seems that the only reason they stop communicating when they die is because they no longer are there. Messages from departed love ones are indeed rare, and when we do get them, they are often speculative, so we question their validity. On top of that, messages from loved ones who have passed to the Other Side generally are obscure.

Culture is another reason for doubt in the western world. Asians are more amenable to the idea of consciousness survival because the culture is more accepting of consciousness that reincarnates and is not trapped in time. Arthur Schopenhauer described this as the primary difference between the West and the East, saying that Europe "is that part of the world which is haunted by the incredible delusion that...his present birth is his first entrance into life."

## ■ Taking the Other Side: Why we believe that our consciousness survives death

For one, we want to. Disappearing completely not only violates our innate survival instincts; also, it violates our sense of purpose. It is rewarding to live a life that has meaning, but a complete cessation of consciousness makes the activities and goals of our lives seem pointless. We want to believe that all the years and effort we spend in living and learning does not dissolve into nothingness when we die. The activities we choose to pursue on earth have a purpose, even if only for entertainment, but spending years of work and enduring unpleasant experiences without meaning is repellent.

Of course, we have an innate desire to live, but a belief in the afterlife extends well beyond our own individual desire to live. Our culture and most dominant religions traditions maintain that what we do on earth will be rewarded or punished after we die. Most of us are taught that an afterlife exists, and we want to feel that we can trust the messengers who taught this to us. Who wants to feel duped, even if unintentionally, by those we love?

More persuasively, there is evidence of consciousness survival. Research on people that remember a past life gives us such evidence, particularly when someone can remember the way around a place never visited in one's current body. Even more convincing is when a person remembers a language never studied in this incarnation. Chris Carter provided several such cases in his book *Science and the Afterlife Experience* (Carter, Science and the Afterlife Experience, 2012, pp. 29-31).

One case was about an Indian girl, Swarnlata Mishra, who was born in 1948. As a child, she began singing songs in a language that was incomprehensible to her parents, and it was later identified as Bengali. She referred to "her house" in a distant Bengali village, to the point that her parents took her at the age of 11 to visit that village. It was 1959, and this was her first visit there, but she not only knew her way around the town but commented on the changes that had happened since she had lived there. Swarnlata recognized twenty people she could identify, always remarking how much they had aged. Two researchers attempted to mislead her in the event that she had gained the knowledge in her current life, but she was not fooled. These researchers verified the evidence and recognized that statements made by Swarnlata were all consistent with what existed in the town in 1939. This was the date of death of a woman, Bija, who Swarnlata had remembered herself to be. If you enjoy such stories of past life memories, I urge you to read Chris Carter's *Science and the Afterlife Experience* (Carter, Science and the Afterlife Experience, 2012)

Research by Dr. Ian Stevenson of the University of Virginia's Division of Perceptual Studies on 2,416 cases of young children who remembered a past life are detailed enough in 60 percent of the cases that the particular past life can be identified in historical records. Often, these children have unusual skills, such as the inexplicable ability to play a musical instrument that was never studied or understand a foreign language used in a past life (Greyson, 2014). With this huge number of verifiable cases, the evidence points to memory as the only realistic explanation. Dr. Bruce Greyson argues that these verifiable past life memories are evidence of consciousness survival, because if consciousness is produced by the brain, memories will not survive the brain's death.

I have touched on one ontological argument in defense of an afterlife, and that is that every physical characteristic of biological life serves some purpose, so spending time learning things while we are in a physical body must be purposeful. This striving to experience and learn even suffering continues as long as we are in the body. Nature does not share its resources wastefully, so why would our bodies experience suffering at the end of our physical existence, when suffering no longer would serve any purpose? Chronic pain at the end of life would have no constructive value unless the payoff of the experience would continue after death. Biologically, physical pain serves the purpose of avoiding things that threaten our health and survival, and it seems that nature would not expend energy on painful lessons as we get older, as there is simply too little payoff for the short duration of existence. Yet some of our most difficult life experiences happen at the end of our bodily lives, when expending resources for so little payoff looks like a violation of the natural order. Since nature abhors expending energy with no payoff, one logical argument is that suffering at this time provides experience and learning for a future beyond the body.

A curious bit of evidence again takes root in probability, which is the broad worldwide pervasiveness of a belief in an afterlife. Human knowledge is grounded in the lived experience of people throughout human history, and this experience has led geographically separate religions around the world to arrive quite independently at very similar conclusions about consciousness survival. This is grounded in experiences that are similar regardless of culture, such as near-death experiences, abilities grounded in past life memories, and verified out-of-body consciousness. Even among widely separated peoples, afterlife beliefs share common features because people everywhere are intuitively able to discern what it true from the lived experiences of people they know. For example, observant people knew that heavy smoking was unhealthy before there were any official studies and pronouncements to that effect—notwithstanding the denial of tobacco companies—through the simple observation that heavy smokers they knew had respiratory problems and illnesses more often than nonsmokers. Likewise, the almost universal belief in life after death by world religions is grounded in centuries of incidents experienced by real people.

Judaism and Buddhism are occasionally mentioned as religions that do not embrace an afterlife, but a bit of digging reveals descriptions of an afterlife in both these traditions. The Jewish Torah is silent regarding an afterlife, but Judaism rabbinic traditions have obvious afterlife overtones. Judaism's Olam Ha Ba (which means "The World to Come") describes a world after the judgment of this world, an ancient rabbinic description of the righteous being rewarded in Gan Eden while the evil are punished in Gehenna or Gehinnom. The Buddhist doctrine of *anatta* directs people to emphasize their earthly existence, but Buddhism nonetheless holds that one may reincarnate. Although the goal of nirvana is sometimes equated with dissolving into nothingness, the supreme release from suffering, Buddhism's *bardo* states describe distinct afterlife experiences.

Most religions speak very directly about a spiritual afterlife or reincarnation and have maintained these conclusions with very little adjustment through millennia of recorded history. If consciousness survival is false, these religions have independently reached wrong conclusions. Very probably, people in all faith traditions have similar real-life experiences that were unusual enough to bring them to the same universal conclusions, as afterlife traditions across religions have substantial common ground to share.

Christianity, in its early days, embraced reincarnation, as evidenced by references in the Gnostic gospels. The concept mostly got swept away in the fourth century by the Council of Nicea, intent on removing conflict among the various strands of Christianity. But Christian scriptures do speak directly of an afterlife. Sometimes it postpones such life until a future second coming of Jesus Christ. But Jesus Christ himself is recorded in the gospels as saying that it continues immediately when he said to one of the men being crucified with him, "Truly, I say to you, today you will be with me in Paradise." (Luke, 23) It is a straightforward conclusion from this direct statement shortly before his death that Christ was saying that consciousness continues immediately after death for himself and others.

I think my own tradition's Christian view of the afterlife displays a lack of imagination, since it emphasizes "the resurrection of the body" to the point of indicating that consciousness requires a body to survive. Despite Christ's promise on the cross about being in paradise that day, Christian tradition today seemingly puts our afterlives on hold, where we rest in peace until the second coming of Christ, when we are said to live again only after reuniting with our bodies.

An emphasis on our rising from the dead on this last day is grounded in the same ideology that is pervasive in scientism—that consciousness needs a body, brain, and nervous system to exist. More likely, consciousness chooses to link temporarily with a body for the sake of enhancing experiences, as food, injuries, sex, and drinks are all experiences heightened by bodily sensations. Perhaps the reason Christ resurrected in a body was to communicate in a way we could understand. A resurrected body that could be seen and touched was a special case for the benefit of our limited perceptions, to best convey that Christ's consciousness continued after death. A resurrected physical body allowed those around Jesus Christ to communicate with him, but it does not mean that a body is necessary for a living consciousness after death.

The biblical accounts of Christ after his resurrection actually give hints that Christ's consciousness was outside his body. One of the curious scriptural aspects of the post-resurrected Christ is that some of those who saw him after the resurrection did not physically recognize him. On the road to Emmaus, the travelers with the post-resurrected Christ felt the power of his words but walked many miles with him before recognizing him "in the breaking of the bread". Perhaps they did not know him while he had walked on earth, but the implication from these stories is that Christ's resurrected body was somehow different from the physical body that was crucified. Christ seems to have reconnected with a version of his body that was changed, such as an etheric body that still maintained the site of the nail and spear wounds from his crucifixion, but was nonetheless a cloak that was unnecessary for his essence.

St. Francis of Assisi was so convinced that we are spirits having a physical experience that he often is reported to have considered the world his cloister and his body as his cell. He himself was so focused on the spirit that his language would befuddle some listeners. For instance, rather than using the Italian equivalent of "I'm cold", tradition says he would phrase things more strangely, such as "my body is cold", implying an awareness of the distinction between his body and his real essence. That is, it was his body that was cold, not himself.

Many of us believe in an afterlife, but I would suspect that few of us have this belief rooted in empirical evidence for consciousness survival. Even with inexplicable past life examples and broadly pervasive religious tenets about the survival of consciousness, the belief we have rarely graduates from a belief to a knowing. There are exceptions, including mediums and near-death experiencers who say they know, but for most of us, including profoundly religious believers, the belief in consciousness after we die is tinged with an inkling of doubt. We shall soon see that survivors of near-death experiences include the most convinced believers in life continuing after physical death.

## ■ Stumbling Blocks for Evidence

There is more evidence for consciousness survival than we may think, but publicizing it is not profitable and has some cultural risks. Spiritual traditions say that looking for evidence of survival reflects human presumption and ignorance, leading us where angels fear to tread. I know that some friends and family dislike my writing about this subject, because a search for evidence fails to toe the line of what a good Catholic is supposed to accept on faith. Even spiritual traditions that believe in heaven, hell or reincarnation do not particularly welcome the evidence of consciousness survival, since it does not rubberstamp the tenets of particular faith traditions. It follows that some of the harshest critics of research on the survival of consciousness research are deeply religious people, who either regard scientific research on the afterlife as invading God's territory or who are upset that the evidence presents a different view of the "afterlife" than what they were taught.

Spiritual traditions prefer to say that consciousness survival is already settled and should be taken on faith, which has its own

CHAPTER

# 13

# OUR BRAINS ARE ANTENNAS—NOT GENERATORS— OF CONSCIOUSNESS

SCIENCE HAS MAINTAINED A BELIEF in brain-generated consciousness while skirting a major stumbling block to this paradigm, which is how the brain, which is composed entirely of matter, can produce consciousness. The concept that matter can produce a totally different entity from itself is a case of spontaneous generation, a theory long discounted by science. If the meat of the brain can produce consciousness, something magical beyond our concept of science is going on. Of course, matter is energy, but consciousness is something beyond electromagnetic energy. Our brains do use energy when we think, which is a case whereby matter in our food is converted into energy. But brain activity and consciousness are conceptually different.

Perhaps the existence of consciousness is no weirder than the Big Bang, which seemingly generated our universe out of nothing. However, if our brains produce the consciousness that so obviously exists, the paradigm must accept that consciousness is somehow spontaneously generated from matter, and the alchemy behind this certainly falls outside our current scientific understanding. We are back at the theoretical, where a designer underlies the origin of consciousness, just as the concept of a designer seems the most rational explanation for the apparent impossibility of the Big Bang.

It is all because this inexplicable thing called consciousness exists. We not only are capable of thinking, but we are capable of thinking about thinking. If the brain does not produce consciousness, where does it come from?

> I don't believe that consciousness is generated by the brain. I believe that the brain is more of a receiver of consciousness.
>
> — Graham Hancock

That the brain *receives* consciousness is a theory that fits well with new evidence. In this explanation, the brain is the mechanical device that, much like a television set, picks up consciousness "waves" that exist independently of our bodies. When the brain is working well, this transmission is good and the consciousness signal is intact. When the brain is injured or otherwise damaged, as in Alzheimer's disease or in drug-induced scenarios, the transmission is likewise altered. In this case, consciousness signals that exist in the universe remain intact, but the brain, like a damaged television set, fails to transmit the consciousness signal adequately. For someone with Alzheimer's disease, for example, the consciousness signal gets garbled and is mostly lost.

This theory posits that consciousness exists independently of the brain and some part of it links up with our brains when we incarnate into bodies. Again using the television analogy, our brains might be said to attune to a particular consciousness frequency. When our physical experience is complete and the brain dies, the receiver that brings the signal to the body has ceased to function. Although a television or brain that has gone kaput no longer receives the broadcast signal, the consciousness signal itself remains intact.

Is this just wishful thinking by theorists who do not like to face death? Actually, this seemingly complex explanation is much cleaner scientifically than assuming that our brains somehow generate consciousness. Our brains and nervous system, at the materialist level of reality, are nothing more than meat. Calling upon meat and electrical current to produce something as esoteric as consciousness is quite an assignment. Science knows that one brain cell cannot form a thought, so what is the mechanism that would allow the emergence of consciousness from a collection of such neurons? On top of that, out-of-body experiences (OBEs) and near-death experiences (NDEs) do occur when brains measure zero activity, yet experiencers were conscious and providing information about their experience and environment that could be verified later.

In the case of Dr. Eben Alexander, his brain was not functioning and was a mass of infectious mush during his near-death experience, but his hyperreal experiences are logical evidence for the existence of verifiable consciousness when brains are effectively dead, confounding the traditional materialist paradigm that consciousness is the result of brain activity. (Alexander, *Proof of Heaven*, 2013).

Evidence that has baffled neuroscience is that a neocortex does not seem to be necessary for a person to have consciousness. Highly intelligent people have been found with practically nothing but cerebral fluid in the brain cavity and almost no neocortex, that part of the brain that materialistic medicine maintains is responsible for thought. Dr. Alexander says that consciousness is stronger when the brain's language centers are disabled, indicating that brain activity actually impedes the experience of consciousness. People who suffered from Alzheimer's for years often become completely lucid shortly before death, another indicator +that the brain hinders the flow of consciousness. That is, when it is powering down before death in these cases, consciousness is enhanced (Greyson, 2014).

From a philosophical perspective, another indicator that consciousness is not simply brain function is that NDErs often mention that they perfectly understood such concepts as "always was", "always will be", and other concepts of infinity in time or space during their NDEs. Oddly, after returning to bodily consciousness, they could no longer understand these concepts that our brains are unable to fathom. Since our brains are limited, they inadequately transmit consciousness to us. During our physical incarnation, consciousness is somehow distorted, likely because our physical brains are incapable of receiving and translating it totally.

Our brains develop in response to the stimuli of our lives, where infinite concepts such as "always was" are irrelevant. Our brains are boxed in to understand limited earthly experiences which do not include infinity, so our synaptic wiring is not designed or adapted to understand it. Even if you have done this many times, try it now. Attempt to figure out the infinity of something, such as the Christian concept that God has always existed and always will exist. Or, simply imagine a universe that has no boundaries, continuing on forever in every direction. Keep expanding the size and time, which must continue expanding forever without limit. Such thinking leaves our brains in an uncomfortable quandary, since our thoughts imagine moving farther and farther through time or space, followed by moving farther again, and then farther *ad infinitum* (!). As for understanding an infinite universe, our brains insist that it not expand forever, since our sensory experience insists on a boundary. Putting an edge on the universe would allow us to conceptualize it by mentally stepping out of it and observing it from the outside. But we know that even if we boxed in the universe to conceptualize it, we are left with another dilemma: what lies outside the box?

In the next chapter, we will look at cases where consciousness leaves the body, focusing on near-death experiences (NDEs) and out-of-body experiences (OBEs). Although our ordinary brains cannot understand infinity, NDErs operating with consciousness and sensory experience that is independent of their bodies report that infinity concepts were perfectly clear during their experiences. This thought experiment implies that consciousness is greater than our brain capacity, and if that is so, it is logically inconsistent that a brain is the source of something grander in design than itself. Consciousness gets glued somehow with our bodies while we live in them, with the brain serving as an imperfect transmitter. Based on the evidence of NDEs, however, pure consciousness that is unfettered by the brain's functioning does grasp and understand concepts like infinity.

CHAPTER

# 14

# LIVING OUTSIDE THE BODY— OUT OF BODY EXPERIENCES AND NEAR-DEATH EXPERIENCES

EARTHLY TRAVEL ENTAILS TAKING YOUR brain and body wherever you go. But out-of-body experiences (OBEs) allow you to go on vacation and leave your brain and body at home (which could cut travel costs appreciably). But seriously, OBEs are travel adventures where one's consciousness separates from the body and travels independently of the body. In every perceptual sense, the OBE feels like movement, complete with visual, auditory, and sensory experience. Unlike a dream, OBEs can happen when one is awake or asleep and they feel intensely real.

The standard materialist objection is that OBEs are simple imagination or hallucination. But this objection utterly fails to explain how an experiencer can get information that he or she did not previously have and could not have obtained by means of the physical senses alone. Yet OBErs often observe real world events in real time at some distant location, and these events can be verified by eyewitnesses who are physically present at the time at that location.

As such, out-of-body experiences open a door of evidence for consciousness survival after death, because during an OBE, one's consciousness is not linked with one's body. The experiencer witnesses events that one's brain and senses are not present to witness perceptually. Since the travel is in real time, OBEs also provide an opportunity for research, since what an out-of-body traveler experiences while consciously outside the body can be verified by real world events happening at that same time. When OBErs witness verifiable events happening at that moment in the "real" world, the traditional argument that consciousness is dependent on the brain and body is nullified, unless this again is a case of super-psi.

Most reported out-of-body experiences begin with a sense of vibration, according to Robert Bruce, an Australian astral dynamics researcher (Bruce, 2009). Although there are variations in the initial stages of an OBE, the experiencer typically feels pulsations or throbbing and may hear vibratory noises before feeling his consciousness lift out of his body. One's consciousness may observe the body from above, but it is not impeded by solid material such as walls, so it can exit the immediate area through them. In many respects, out-of-body experiences resemble hyper-real dreams, with the all-important distinguishing characteristic of being physically awake and able to perceive actual events happening at that moment somewhere else in the universe.

For several reasons, out-of-body experiencers scoff at assertions that OBEs are fundamentally glorified dreams or hallucinations. They say that OBEs are hyper-real, perceptually much clearer than the comparatively drab ambiance of dreams, which lack the overwhelming sense of reality characteristic of OBEs. Vision and hearing are perceptually much clearer than in a dream. It is hypothesized that OBErs witness a truer state of consciousness, above and beyond the day-to-day consciousness that is dampened by our brain's inability to collect and transmit information perfectly.

Since experiencers are not seeing with their physical eyes or hearing with their physical ears, OBErs almost universally report that their visual acuity and hearing are greatly enhanced during the experience, as are all their senses. This is particularly true if the person's bodily senses are handicapped or compromised, because sights and sounds in the OBE are far clearer than the sensory perceptions normally experienced. One OBEr with highly myopic eyesight reported seeing a highway sign in the distance during his OBE. The sign was too far from the location of his awareness for him to have read it with his physical eyes, yet he was able to read it clearly in his OBE. This was a real highway sign, so real world witnesses could match what the sign actually said with what the OBEr reported it to say. Such experiences are especially convincing when the OBEr has never physically been at the location encountered in the OBE and, nonetheless, the contents of these sign messages are independently confirmed. Ring and Cooper's research noted that blind people who had experienced an OBE or NDE reported veridical perceptions that could only be described as visual, as their perceptions would be otherwise impossible (Ring K. a., 1999).

Curiously, a significant number of OBErs have reported witnessing fires or explosions, and a need to act may underlie why their OBE was initiated. These events happened while their bodies were elsewhere, but the consciousness of the OBEr observed them in real time.

Does this confirm that consciousness exists independently of the body? That is certainly a strong likelihood, but we have visited the possibility that OBEs represent a form of super-psi rather than an actual relocation of consciousness. If that is the case, the OBE presents a hyper-real illusion of travel, but the consciousness remains with a body that is psychically picking up information not available to the five major senses. Either way, OBEs represent something beyond physical sensory experience, since real world events witnessed during OBEs are repeatedly verified after the fact. OBEs at least provide intriguing evidence that our consciousness can perceive things in ways that the material scientist would claim to be impossible.

If OBEs are more than super-psi and the information they deliver is coming from consciousness separated from the body, the important point that logically follows is that consciousness does not necessarily need to be attached to a body, leaving it free to survive and move on when a body dies. Although veridical evidence from OBEs is common, much of it is dead on arrival when read by materialist scientists, who dismiss it based on that paradigm of reality that does not allow the possibility. Over time, mounting evidence eventually will crumble the paradigm that cannot explain it.

# ■ A Step Farther

Although OBEs open a door, near-death experiences (NDEs) provide more extensive hints that human consciousness survives death. NDEs are transcendent super-real experiences from people who are close to death, and in many cases clinically dead, yet return to physical life to relay these experiences. Experiences vary, but often contain characteristic elements such as an indescribable light, meeting and communicating with loved ones who have died, and an intense desire not to leave the experience. Although NDEs have been reported over 1,000 years ago (Baumann, 2001, p. 17), they had long been ignored or suppressed, again passed off as simply the hallucinations of a brain winding down, but research by Raymond Moody, Kenneth Ring, Janice Miner Holden, P.M.H. Atwater and others since the mid-1970s have provided us with intriguing implications of these transcendent experiences. Every year, nearly 200,000 people in the United States have a near-death experience and although the statistics vary, the International Association of Near Death Studies reports that more than two-thirds of them involve a spiritual experience (About Near-Death Experiences, 2014). Words seem to fail NDErs when they attempt to describe these spiritual experience(s). A child may have described her NDE best, remarking that "We are stuffed full of love, like God is." (Atwater, Dying to Know You: Proof of God in the Near Death Experience, 2014)

NDEs are more convincing and illustrative evidence of consciousness survival than OBEs on several counts. For one, in hundreds of studies at the University of Virginia's School of Medicine, 42 percent of NDEs included visits with a deceased person. Often the experiencer did not know the person to be dead at the time of the NDE. This included a case of a young boy who was told by his college-age sister that he must leave his NDE and return to his body. His sister had just been killed in an automobile accident, and at the time of the boy's NDE, he and his family had not yet been notified of her death (Greyson, 2014). NDEs usually are unbelievably intense, representing a realm of reality that supersedes human explanation. Consequently, they generally are life-changing events that can totally alter a person's perception of life and its purpose. These almost indescribable encounters often turn atheists into convinced theists, or at least believers that unbounded love pervades a realm beyond our earthly existence.

Nurses and hospice workers have heard their share of NDE accounts but because their training did not address NDEs, they were "whispering in the shadows" about them (Janssen, 2014). I have heard nurses say that they generally were afraid to speak about NDE stories until the prevalence of these phenomena became more apparent. Eventually, the evidence has become overwhelming enough that in 2013, the University of California at Riverside awarded a grant for scientific research of NDEs of heart attack patients (Bachrach, 2014, p. 229).

Serious research of near-death experiences is hindered, however, because NDEs cannot be ordered up on demand. As with OBEs, again we find skeptics postulating that near-death experiences are merely the last gasp perceptions of a dying brain, adaptive machinations by which our bodies make the process of dying less scary to our survival instincts. These observers argue that NDEs are not evidence of consciousness survival, but merely anoxia as our brains power down. A 2013 study suggests that neuronal high frequency gamma oscillations that precede flat-line EEGs in a dying brain could explain the hallucinatory characteristics of an NDE. However, such theories remain hard pressed to explain how near-death experiences and out-of-body experiences often include those veridical perceptions of events somewhere else in the world. Hallucinations simply do not observe actual nonlocal real-world events accurately. Distinguishing between NDEs and ordinary experience, Michael Sabom's studied the accuracy of people describing their resuscitation procedures after surgery. He found no errors among people who had experienced an NDE during surgery, but when he asked survivors without an NDE how they had been resuscitated, 80 percent of the answers were incorrect. (Greyson, 2014)

A man by the name of Yuri was struck by a car and found himself "surrounded by the light" of an NDE (Baumann, 2001, p. 9). His consciousness left his body and journeyed to his neighbors' house. Even though he could not talk with anyone there, he discovered in amazement that he could nonverbally communicate with their newborn baby. The baby was very distressed and distinctly told Yuri that his arm hurt, whereby Yuri was able to see a twisted and broken bone in the baby's arm. After Yuri was later revived and relayed this communication to his neighbors, they took their child to a doctor, who confirmed by X-ray that the baby did have a broken arm. In another case of veridical evidence, Tony Cicoria had a near-death experience after lighting struck him. Although his body was lying outside on the ground, his peaceful awareness traveled up a flight of stairs to check on his family. He was surprised to see his wife painting the children's faces, a rather uncommon event which was nonetheless verified to be what she was doing when he was struck by lightning. (Cicoria & Cicoria, 2014, p. 4).

Such anecdotal stories of NDEs abound, but Michael Sabom, M.D., conducted systematic research in the 1980s, gathering and documenting a database of intriguing veridical evidence on reported NDEs (Sabom, 1998). One case was relayed by a woman I shall call Stella. Several physicians in an emergency room were feverishly working on Stella's body when her consciousness rose up and hovered near the ceiling of the room. Her brain scans registered no cognitive activity at the time, indicating unconsciousness or death, but she clearly heard the frustrated conversations of the physicians attempting to revive her. Meanwhile, her sight and hearing were positioned at a location near the ceiling, even though her physical eyes and ears remained on the operating table. Suddenly, her consciousness unceremoniously slammed back into her body, and she survived her touch with death. Later, while recovering in a separate room, she reported to the staff that they should clean the top of a light fixture in the emergency room because there were two dead roaches on the top of this fixture. The staff pooh-poohed her imagination, defensively pointing out that they ran an antiseptic hospital that did not include roach carcasses lying around in the emergency room. They believed she was reporting a postoperative hallucination or dream, since she was confined to her room and had no access to the top of a light fixture hanging high in the emergency room. Stella was determined about what she had seen, so to allay her persistent requests, a ladder was set up next to the light fixture over the operating table. Behold, two long-dead roach carcasses were found on top of the light fixture. Such demonstrable experiences, although anecdotal, happen frequently enough to trump coincidence and override explanations grounded in simple hallucinations.

One of the more popular examples of a veridical NDE was reported by Kimberley Clark in 1984, regarding a migrant worker I will call Anna who was visiting friends in Seattle when she suffered a heart attack. Anna was rushed to Harborview Hospital where she had another cardiac arrest, ostensibly rendering her unconscious. But her consciousness hovered outside the hospital and was attracted to a single tennis shoe on an exterior ledge off the third floor of the north side of the building. She studied the shoe in detail and later described it as having obvious scuffs over the little toe and one of its laces jammed underneath the heal. Anna described this experience in detail to Kimberley Clark, her nurse, and a shoe exactly matching this description was found on the very ledge Maria had said. The shoe could not be seen from the ground, and the difficult process to recover the shoe discovered that the only perspective in which someone could have seen the shoe with the details she described would be if the person had been hovering outside the building (Ring & Lawrence, Summer, 1993).

Another corroborated case from 1982 was reported by Joyce Harmon, a Hartford hospital nurse resuscitating a patient while wearing plaid shoelaces she had just purchased and worn that day. An unconscious female patient was on the operating table and could not have seen Joyce's shoes with her physical eyes, especially while unconscious the entire time. This woman later reported that she had watched her resuscitation from above her body, and upon seeing Harmon, the patient said, "Oh, you're the one with the plaid shoelaces." (Ring & Lawrence, Summer, 1993)

Judy Bachrach relays the experience of Pam Reynolds Lowery, who later imparted conversations she overheard between medical personnel while undergoing a medical procedure. She accurately described the look and sound of an intricate medical instrument she witnessed, even though her physical ears had been blocked and her eyes taped shut during the entire procedure (Bachrach, 2014, p. 228). On top of that, her consciousness had been completely anesthetized. Regardless, she accurately saw the instrument with something other than her physical eyes.

Visual reports from NDErs who are physically blind are even more fascinating. Kenneth Ring and Sharon Cooper's research of NDEs and OBEs included 14 cases in which the experiencer was blind since birth. Even though these people were not familiar with visual sight, nine reported sight during their NDEs. Based on reports, these sensory experiences were foreign to them but had all the hallmark signs of physical vision. (Carter, Science and the Near-Death Experience: How Consciousness Survives Death, 2010, pp. 230-231). This is hardly surprising given that NDErs have long reported 360-degree visual awareness enveloping their bodies, displaying abilities such as "eyes in the back of the head". Greatly enhanced vision, hearing, and understanding are typical in NDEs and OBEs, and include perceptions described as more real than real. People who have been deaf since childhood have reported the ability to hear sounds during an NDE. They were able to identify the sense of hearing because they remembered what it was like to hear during their childhood.

I have not experienced a transcendent near-death experience myself, but given my talks with people who have, I accept the reality of NDEs at a "gut level", based on their deeply honest beliefs and emotional reactions. I recently attended a long afternoon meeting of our local chapter of IANDS (the International Association for Near Death Studies), and the stories people shared were striking. In sharing their experiences, normal-looking men and women who had experienced an NDE quite recently often broke down to gut-wrenching weeping. The reason for their tears was rather amazing to attendees who have not personally experienced an NDE. Through their tears, they were asking "Why me?" The question was not bemoaning a close brush with death but was a deep lament that they had been told to leave the NDE and return to physical life. They found it overbearingly difficult to return to normal earthly existence after being enveloped in the divine and indescribable love they had experienced. They all said that their preference was to remain on that other side of existence, even though this meant dying physically.

The woman sitting next to me revealed that she had two children whom she loved immensely, but the love she experienced in her NDE was "thousands of times greater" than any love she knew in daily life on earth. Although she spoke of great love for her children and the need they had for her, she would have decided "in a heartbeat"—had she been given the choice—not to come back to her bodily existence on earth. She and other recent NDErs shared their anguish in not understanding what was so important on earth that they had to come back. If it was not their time to pass, why were they given a glance at an experience that was so overwhelming that words are inadequate to describe it, only to be told that they had to return to their bodies? Attendees who had their NDEs many years ago collectively identified with these emotions from recent NDErs, but since they had time to adapt back to earthly life since their NDE, they helped the newbies with their feelings. To a person, these NDErs were absolutely convinced that life continues after death.

Beyond this smattering of personal stories, agreement about the existence of an afterlife among large numbers of NDErs is pervasive. The overwhelming agreement is so statistically unlikely that even traditional academia, long afraid of being accused of nonscientific thinking, has taken baby steps to research what lies behind this highly peculiar cohesion among NDErs. What remains baffling to sampling statisticians and numbers nerds like me is the lack of doubt among large samples of people who have experienced NDEs. Highly unusual statistical oddities get my attention and early NDE research revealed the oddest sampling data I have seen. In a typical survey or large groups of people, the normal distribution rules in statistics. This simply means that large numbers of people share similar experiences while unusual experiences on one extreme or the other are experienced by progressively smaller numbers of people.

When plotted, the statistician sees a bell-shaped curve referred to as a normal distribution.

Here is the statistical oddity of NDErs. Raymond Moody's research on hundreds of NDErs in the 1980s revealed that 100 percent of the NDErs reported a belief in God and an afterlife after their experience, regardless of their beliefs before the NDE. Statistically, I would call it a near-miracle when a researcher finds 100 percent agreement from hundreds of individuals on anything subjective. I could believe 100 percent if the sampled group was comprised of only a few people. However, with so many individual differences, asking hundreds of people whether 1 plus 1 equals 2 would not find 100 percent agreement. This is the only serious study of hundreds of people where I recall seeing 100 percent agreement on a subjective question. I recall sharing that statistic with the Jesuits when I was considering entering the Jesuit religious order, as that statistic was a powerful piece of evidence to me that NDEs represent divine transcendence at work.

More recently, a few exceptions to this 100 percent have popped up in the research, but when studying those NDErs who do not embrace a belief in the afterlife, these were people, almost to a person, did not have a transcendental NDE. What they experienced would better be described as a close brush with death. That is, although they may have been at death's door, their experiences were limited to fear and an instinct for physical survival. That is, they did not share even one of the transcendent NDE patterns delineated by Raymond Moody and others (such as a tunnel, bright light, loving entity, an indescribable sense of love and acceptance, etc.). Researchers still find that when true NDErs asked about the existence of an afterlife, the responses spike exceptionally in the center, replicating the extremely unusual statistical pattern. Even those with negative NDEs (which Dr. Janice Miner Holden pegs at about 12 percent), are almost unanimously convinced that there is more to life than our physical existence.

Increasingly, the general consensus among health professionals is moving away from the opinion that an NDE is a mental hallucination, drug reaction, or consequence of oxygen-deprivation. Although Olaf Blanke *et al.* stimulated parts of the hypothalamus, hippocampus, amygdala, and frontal lobe of the brain to simulate the sensations of a near-death experience, the life-changing transcendental effects of a true NDE did not ensue (Blanke, Landis, Spinelli, & Seeck, 2004). As NDEs are more widely reported, such "explanatory" theories grounded in brain physiology are inadequate because many NDEs happen when the brain is flat-lined. Stimulating any part of the brain at that time is inconsequential (Caudill, 2012, p. 132). Dr. L. Stafford Betty of California State University at Bakersfield researched multiple NDEs from avowed atheists and others whose brains were "flat-lined" at the time of their NDE, but they reported vivid experiences (Betty, 2006). These were brains that were not shutting down, but had already shut down, with no cognitive function at all. Even hardcore scientists agree that hallucinations require active brain function. The fact that there is any consciousness at all when the cognitive parts of the brain are not working says that something extraordinary and otherworldly is at play. Also, purely physical explanations do not explain the veridical NDEs that provide information that could not be obtained by the senses alone. Whether veridical NDEs are a sign of consciousness survival or an example of super psychic awareness, traditional science is faced with a paranormal event begging for an explanation.

Dr. Eben Alexander, the neurosurgeon and author of *Proof of Heaven*, points out that his own medical training previously had convinced him that NDEs were purely physical, but his own NDE blasted holes in that theory (Alexander, Proof of Heaven: A Neurosurgeon's Journey into the Afterlife, *2012*). He had no measurable brain activity during the time, but his NDE included an encounter with a beautiful young woman whom he did not know. She guided him during his transcendent experience, and Eben later discovered that this woman was his sister, who had died a couple of years before. To be met by a deceased sister during an NDE is not unusual, but because Eben had been given up for adoption as a child, he was not even aware that he had a sister. After his NDE, Dr. Alexander met his biological parents for the first time since his infancy, and he was shown photographs of his deceased blood sister. To his amazement, the woman who had guided him on his NDE was undoubtedly the same woman pictured in those photographs.

A very common characteristic of NDEs is meeting loved ones who have died. They appear in the physical bodies they had on earth, although usually younger in appearance and dressed in recognizable clothing. The visions are of people who are deceased, rather than a mishmash of random living and dead people. This is a formidable argument that NDEs are not mere hallucinations. If they were, we would expect these visions to include people who are still physically alive, but according to L. Stafford Betty's research, they do not. Hallucinations would have no way of sorting out who has passed on from who has not, especially when the person having the NDE does not consciously know that information. In deathbed visions where a dying person was accompanied by living persons, the dying person could distinguish between those who were physically living and those who were dead (Betty, 2006).

Universal near-death experiences would provide strong evidence of consciousness survival and build on faith, but NDEs are far from universal. In fact, most people who survive a brush with death do not remember having a near-death experience. Research shows that a relatively small percentage of people who recover from a close encounter with death (10 to 15 percent, according to Dr. Janice Miner Holden) can recall having an NDE (Holden, 2014). Do the others not recall an experience because they did not have one, or did they simply not remember having one? That is not unknown, since we do know the reason NDEs happen.

In a conscious universe, not remembering an NDE could be by design, particularly when the person does not die at that time. I suggest that the lack of universal near-death memories keeps us guessing what they are and how they arrive. We are on shaky ground in trying to study the survival of something we fundamentally do not understand, but as well as it can be grasped, communication with departed loved ones is a signpost of consciousness continuing after death. When messages can be ascertained to a degree that overrides coincidence (based on a statistically significant correlation), we have science pointing in the same direction as world religions—that our consciousness somehow exists beyond the matter of our brains and outside our bodies.

# 15

# COMMUNICATING WITH THOSE WHO HAVE DIED

"...between us and you there is a great chasm fixed, so that those who wish to come over from here to you will not be able, and that none may cross over from there to us."
Gospel of Luke 16:26

CAN WE LEARN TO REACH across the chasm and communicate directly with loved ones who have died? Many anomalies are best explained by consciousness living on after death, but the relative lack of communication from those who have passed away remains a big question mark. Communicating with someone who has died can be the best evidence that our true selves live on after physical death.

Here is an understatement with near-universal acceptance: Death puts a crimp in communication between people. The Christian scriptures speak of a chasm that separates those living in the body from those who have departed. Those same scriptures never say that communication is impossible, but the word "chasm" obviously points out that communication will be far more difficult after someone has died. For most of us, even the deeply religious believers in life after death, we have a particularly difficult time with this.

Communication with loved ones who have died is rare for most of us and nonexistent for many. The lack of communication is a dominating reason why questions remain that our consciousness survives death. With evidence signaling some form of consciousness survival, it remains a valid question why communication breaks down after death. If our departed loved ones simply talked to us more clearly, that would be all the evidence we need to know that our consciousness lives on after we die. But because communication is so fragmented when someone dies, we are left with a huge snag in the evidence for consciousness survival. If someone loved us dearly on earth and remains consciously alive, why is there not more communication? Do they forget us? Or, since the standards for communication have changed, do they not know how to get through to us? Are we the problem? It could well be that they are sending messages that we fail to pick up or understand. Or is there something else that prevents straightforward communication?

Obviously, these pages will not contain definitive answers to these burning questions, but I can speculate based on those fragments of evidence that we have. It cannot be overstated how frustrating and painful this unfortunate state of communication breakdown is for someone wanting just a simple sign from a lost loved one. Even when we get a message, the lack of clarity leaves us in doubt about its authenticity. It seems that we are living a carefully crafted excursion in the body in which we are given just enough evidence of life's continuance to motivate us, yet we remain burdened with lingering doubt that our spiritual urgings are imaginary feelings that will disappear when our earthly stay wraps up.

The most likely reason that clear communication seems to stop when someone we love passes away is our failure to recognize that the method of communication obviously has to change. Do not blame your departed loved ones. They may be as confused about how to communicate with us as we are confused about communicating with them! We can only guess how much ability we will have to send messages to our survivors when we die.

For starters, a body is essential for communication on earth. The physical body is, after all, the body of physics, while a discarnate spirit by definition has no fleshly body that can use the laws of physics to communicate. Because discarnate entities are pure energy, they no longer have physical voices, arms, ears, eyes and bodies. It would be easy for us to communicate if people who passed on manifested themselves in bodies that could talk and listen or sign, but we cannot expect messages we can hear with our ears or visions we see with our eyes. Even apparitions generally are silent.

NDErs claim that communication during an NDE is totally nonverbal. Experiencers fail to find words to describe how it works, but the best earthly word may be telepathic. For most of us, we use vocal cords and language designed for communicating through an earthly atmosphere that transfers sound, but once free of the body, the discarnate must adapt to a different method. Once out of the body, a discarnate person no longer uses air passing over vocal cords and can no longer make audible sounds. The discarnate no longer has hands and movements to communicate, no muscles to provide tactile messages, and no means to provide messages through taste or smell. Dr. Judy Beischel, in her book *From the Mouths of Mediums (Volume 1)* notes that discarnate spirits must learn to communicate with energy, and they may not necessarily be good at it (Beischel, 2014), location 785). Once again, people expecting a message from a deceased loved one may be getting a message, but are not recognizing telepathy because they are "used to dealing with physicality and not pure energy." (Beischel, 2014), location 848) A loophole argument made by those who claim that after-death communication is not real is that a message from someone with an unusual trait of speech on earth should have that same trait on the other side. It is assumed that this trait of speech should be recognizable in any communication from the deceased.

Such patterns often occur in mediumship as the discarnate person uses characteristic earthly habits to convince the receiver that the message is authentic. In most cases, however, researchers and receivers note that the vocabulary of the message is quite generic.

With this in mind, I recently received a couple of messages from my deceased friend David Austin, whose English language vocabulary was the largest of anyone I knew. He loved language and had an extensive knowledge of Latin roots, so he would pepper his conversations with rare and uncommon words, leaving me busy with online and smartphone dictionaries when he sent me e-mails. However, in the two messages I received from him since his death, there was no new vocabulary to surprise me. The content of the messages surprised me a bit, which was very typical for David, so the content itself made the authenticity of the messages quite convincing, but the messages came to me in language that sounded like my own words. That made me suspicious. The messages would have been conclusively convincing had he hit me with new words that would send me to the dictionary. Should I doubt the authenticity of these messages because they did not contain David's esoteric vocabulary?

I asked for spiritual guidance on this suspicion. I was told no, and here is the reason I was given. As NDErs attest during their experiences, messages are not verbal but telepathic and symbolic. No words are exchanged to convey crystal clear meaning. So if and when we get messages from someone who has passed on, our own brains put these telepathic messages into words we understand, so we will not get telepathic translations in words we do not have in our own vocabulary. We are receiving wordless communication from the other side. Our minds will understand the message, and when we convert it into words for our memory, our brains find the best words we know to deliver the message. Earthly languages are an earthly creation and are not fundamental on the other side. If they were, we would already know them when we are born on earth.

Instead, they are designed for communication with human anatomy. Except for cases of previous life memories, such as that of Swarnlata Mishra already discussed, that is not the case. The different means of communication between us and the other side is perhaps the primary reason that afterlife communication is so difficult and why the Christian scriptures tell us that physical death separates us by a chasm.

# ■ Time

. . . . . . . . . . . . . . . . . . . . . . . . . . . . . . . . . . . . . . . . . . . . . . . . .

A second culprit impeding communication with departed loved ones is time. While we are in our bodies, we live in a world of space and time—the dimensions of physics and the physical universe. Since we cannot travel near the speed of light (which becomes practically impossible for bodies due to the inconceivable amount of energy required and the killing acceleration that would be necessary), time moves in one direction and at virtually the same rate from our births until our deaths. Since our consciousness is usually glued to the body while we are physically alive, our awareness also lives in a world of dimensions and time. And just as we could not understand temperature if it was always the same, our experiential understanding of time is a flow that always moves in the same direction at the same rate. We have no practical understanding how to deal with time when it does not.

However, the evidence from near-death survivors and out-of-body experiencers is that time disappears when our consciousness leaves its physical state. Those on the other side do not perceive time the way we do, and based on reported statements from mediums, they do not experience time at all. That may be difficult to comprehend, but physics tells us that the state of timelessness actually exists in our universe in the form of light. As mentioned, all light that has been traveling since the Big Bang remains at the same moment of time as the Big Bang, according to Einstein's relativity. This is because traveling at the speed of light causes the passage of time to stop. Regardless of whether discarnate spirits share this timeless property of light, time outside the physical world is perceived differently, if it is perceived at all.

The peculiar property of timelessness cannot be experienced in our physical bodies, but when NDErs leave the body and interact with the light, their consciousness is released from the restrictions of time. This timeless property and universal connectivity with light would arguably release us to be everywhere at the same time. NDErs often report entire detailed life reviews in an instant, an instant in which they deeply sensed even detailed feelings of all the people they interacted with. So, it is little wonder that spirits passing out of the body do not share our sense of time, which may be at the root of our frustration in communication with departed souls. I love a story shared in recordings by the late psychic Sylvia Browne regarding to her father's death. Sylvia dearly loved her father and often mentioned that she had a close relationship with him, so she was certain that her psychic sensitivity would allow their relationship to continue after he died. Yet, for more than a year after his death, she got no message from him, which bothered her greatly. Then the spirit of her father made a connection with her, and she was overjoyed to get it. Still, because she had waited so long to get a message from him, she pointedly asked him something on the lines of "Where the hell have you been?"

"What do you mean?" he inquired. "I just got here."

Yes, our concept of time disappears when we cross over. Sylvia's dad did not realize that he had been in the spirit world for more than one earthly year. So another reason most of us rarely get messages from our loved ones after they pass on is because our experience of many years may seem like an instant to them. They may not be ignoring us, even through dozens of earthly years. They simply are no longer living in our world of time and overlook how the passage of earthly time still affects us.

# ▇ Electromagnetic Messages

Electrical and electronic messages are probably the most common form of afterlife communication. As is typical for paranormal investigation, why and how discarnate spirits use electricity and electronics to give us messages is unknown. But given countless stories over decades, it is one apparent way that the chasm between corporeal life and the afterlife is crossed.

There has been research on electric and telephone contact from deceased individuals for many decades, including a 1915 account of a wireless telegraph producing messages in Morse code when no messages had been sent, even when the receiving antenna was disconnected. Likewise, there have been accounts of unusual telephone messages from the dead for nearly as long as telephones have existed. A book published in the 1920s was called "Voices from Beyond the Telephone". It was written by a Brazilian author, Carlos Ramos, who provided stories of unexplained telephonic communication from someone who was physically dead. In a more systematic work published in 1979, Raymond Bayless and D. Scott Rogo provided the results of a two-year investigation entitled *Phone Calls from the Dead*. Recent books on the subject have been written by Wendy Brenner and Callum E. Cooper, an English doctoral candidate who pursues the many possible sources for such communication without emotional attachment, providing an opportunity for unbiased research.

# ■ Frustrating Brevity

. . . . . . . . . . . . . . . . . . . . . . . . . . . . . . . . . . . . . . . . . . . . . . . . .

We should be thankful for whatever communication from the other side we get, even if the communication is more subtle than we would like. One of my first cousins, for example, is convinced that she saw her recently deceased husband come to her with a huge smile, which was his trademark expression for her. He came to tell her that everything was OK, and although she was convinced that it was a message from him, her description of it hit me as woefully abbreviated. If he had the ability to give that message to his beloved spouse on earth, it seems he could add a few words and a bit more time of comfort and encouragement. I suppose we must remember that words and time are two concepts of earth—and not the other side.

More often than not, history records that manifestations from someone who has passed are short in duration. The only communication may be that all is well, followed by some indication that the departed entity must quickly get back to the other side. Sometimes there is a message that there will be no further contact. Talking to our departed loved ones in our prayers and meditations is not as comforting as a tête-à-tête would be, and we rarely are sure if our message is getting through. The most convincing evidence we are left with in these difficult two-way attempts is that communication between the realms of earthly existence and existence in the beyond is complex indeed.

The scriptural chasm separating those living in the body from those on the other side emphatically indicates that communication will be difficult for those who have departed—and difficult for us as well.

CHAPTER

# 16

# MEDIUMSHIP AND A WHOLE
# NEW LANGUAGE

COMMUNICATING WITH THE DEAD SEEMS to require special skills, as discarnate spirits no longer have vocal cords and bodies to manipulate physical objects of communication. Few of us have honed these special skills. That is why we recognize certain people with these talents and label them professionally as mediums. One piece of solid evidence is that mediums get better at their craft with practice, indicating that some sort of true communication is going on. It also verifies that mediumship is a skill, implying that we are all candidates that have some mediumship ability. We simply need practice to gain proficiency. The Arthur Findlay College in the United Kingdom is an educational institution that has long taken this perspective and maintains that mediumship can be trained. Arthur Findlay may be the only professional school in the western world with an entire curriculum for mediumship and a solid reputation for successfully training mediums.

Doubters regarding the reality of mediumship undoubtedly outnumber doubters about the existence of psi. For a materialist mindset, talking to the dead is farther along the road of folly than extrasensory messages among the living. On top of that, mediumship suffers a lousy reputation, having been riddled with fraudulent goings-on through the centuries. The landscape was littered with entertainers who played up the public's interest in rousing a deceased specter, even if they lacked any genuine intent to be real. Tricksters had no need to be real mediums and very probably did not even believe in what they were claiming to do. In the late nineteenth century, most of these disingenuous performers insisted on conducting their craft in dark shadows, reveling in a suspenseful ambience. Although such carnival-like shams were not serious mediumship, such fake practices stained the reputation of true mediumship, linking it to a circus-like atmosphere that intelligent witnesses never took seriously.

Mediumship also suffers from a widespread cultural belief that communicating with the dead is impossible, especially if one does not believe that the dead still exist. One of the pervasive arguments made by those who doubt the survival of consciousness is precisely the one already mentioned, that people who loved us on earth quickly stop communicating with us when they die. Although there is some communication, these objections are valid stumbling blocks to belief, since we know that people who pray for a message may never get one, at least not in a form they recognize. This real and serious issue will be addressed, but for now, true mediums are quick to tell us that, despite the apparent silence, many discarnate spirits are quite determined to break through with a message and will hound whoever has the genuine skills to pick it up. The breakdown in communication is probably not because they no long exist or because they no longer care about us, but because both the sender and receiver must learn a different way to communicate. The medium John Holland often mentions that discarnate spirits "line up" with him to get a message across to their loved ones on earth.

Most mediums are convinced that they are communicating with the dead, and from a scientific perspective, genuine mediums are getting information. But getting information, even if it is unknown to anyone alive, does not prove that consciousness survives, as there are those alternate possibilities about the source of the messages. I have already mentioned one of the most prevalent theories—that the medium is not communicating with a discarnate spirit but is picking up information through extrasensory perception. That is, the medium may be drawing information psychically from energy fields left behind while a discarnate spirit was alive. A second theory also relies on psychic information but says that the messages received by a medium are psychically picked up from the departed's living relatives, loved ones, and friends still living on earth. These people know information about the deceased, and the medium is psychically reading their minds. The huge flaw with this theory, however, is that mediums sometimes get information that no one alive knows. Mediums often deliver messages intended for someone who simply does not understand it, or the message may contain information not recognizable to anyone alive. Intended recipients may even deny what a medium is saying and tell the medium that the message is wrong. Every experienced medium knows this routine occurrence but also knows that eventual verification is likely. The marvelous truth is that recipients of a message often discover the truth of the message later. When no one alive knows the information the medium has received, it is extremely doubtful that the medium is simply reading the minds of the deceased's acquaintances and loved ones.

Afterlife communication that profoundly alters what is believed diminishes the notion that the medium is simply picking up psychic information from living persons. Even precognition of what people would know in the future is ruled out if they would never have learned the information without the message from beyond. When no one alive knows the information the medium is relaying, the simplest explanation, using the theory of Occam's razor, is that the medium is indeed communicating with a departed spirit who is still alive in a discarnate state. This reveals nothing about how messages get through, which may be very complex, but it is a link of evidence that consciousness survives death. John Holland is one of those mediums who confidently claims to *know* that consciousness survives after death. And given his verifiable mediumship witnessed by thousands, he has the evidence to move from a belief to a knowing that consciousness survives death.

Anecdotal stories are interesting and convincing to the mediums who receive them, but is there any serious research on mediumship? Fortunately, yes. Statistical studies have been employed for years, but as with psi, the results tell us that the messages are real but the origin of the messages is speculative and inconclusive. Determining if apparitions represent real communication with the dead was a reason for the formation of the British Society for Psychical Research way back in 1882. An American counterpart of this group formed two years later, and both pursued scientific research into apparitions and other psychic phenomena. The British organization was founded "free of prejudice or prepossession", and interestingly, some of their own members were skeptical but curious.

Skeptics in our time can explore the statistical results on mediumship reported in 2002 by Gary Schwartz of the University of Arizona (Schwartz G., 2002). Schwartz's careful and detailed experiments compared the accuracy of professional mediums with a randomly selected sample of people. In the extensive research project, a random person typically was accurate about 30 percent of the time when confronted with questions about the appearance, personality, cause of death, and hobbies of an unfamiliar person who had died. Talented mediums who were asked these same questions about a person they did not know averaged an accuracy rate of about 85 percent when they sought answers from the deceased individual. Consistent results at this level of accuracy are effectively impossible for a large sample of people unless real communication is going on with someone. The strongest hypothesis is that mediumship is real communication with a person living on the "Other Side" of existence, once again placing science face to face with the arena of religion and spirituality.

More recently, the Windbridge Institute for Applied Research in Human Potential in Tucson, Arizona, has dedicated itself to tackling scientific research on mediumship (www.windbridge.org). Since its inception in 2008, Windbridge has studied the content and accuracy of messages from multiple mediums, and although these messages certainly are subject to error, consistent results are convincingly due to something well beyond fraud or lucky guesses. The Windbridge Institute's research has concentrated on the accuracy of mediums who receive messages mentally without any form of possession by a departed spirit. Still, some mediums feel that some form of possession can occur and even may help the process. When it occurs, these mediums report an ability to maintain control of the process and stop this possession if they want. (Beischel, 2014)

The unfortunate reality is that messages from discarnate spirits are often vague, difficult to interpret, and so unobtrusive and quiet that those of us still lumbering around in a body miss the messages entirely, even if we want them. One culprit is that messages from departed souls—for some reason—are often highly symbolic. It requires skill to interpret the symbolic language, explaining why mediums get more accurate with practice. If we are not adept enough ourselves to receive and understand a message, the conduit of a medium provides an opportunity for a discarnate spirit who wants to communicate with us. That is why discarnate spirits will line up at a mediumship reading to get a message across to those of us not experienced enough to pick up these messages without help.

Anyone who has witnessed a public mediumship event knows that the medium sometimes will misinterpret these symbolic messages. Such mistakes actually can make the messages more authentic, because they provide an opportunity for the true humanity of the discarnate spirit to come through. When the spirit attempts to correct the medium, he or she displays all the emotions that were characteristic of that person while alive on earth. At such times, mediums may comment on the personality of the message giver, using words such as feisty, sweet, demanding, retiring, or vivacious.

Mediums say that the meaning of the symbols they receive is like learning a new language. Here is yet another reference to John Holland, whom I mention because he communicates so successfully about being an intermediary message transmitter. For him, a message received may be visual or auditory, but deciphering the meaning accurately has required years of practice. More than once, I have heard him use the example of Niagara Falls and its symbolic meaning. He has learned that when he gets an image of Niagara Falls in a mediumship event, it is a symbolic reference (for him) that means Canada (Holland, 2008). It may refer to something happening anywhere in Canada, such as in the Canadian Yukon or in Vancouver, which makes little geographic sense for a place that is a continent away from Niagara Falls. No matter. In John's mediumship, when a discarnate spirit gives him the symbol of Niagara Falls, he knows the message has something to do with Canada.

It is important to note that these symbolic meanings are not universal for everyone, so another medium may get the image of a maple leaf for Canada and interpret Niagara Falls to mean drowning or New York or getting married or countless other possibilities. But these symbols appear to be consistent for an individual, so Niagara Falls will have the same meaning the second, third, and fourth time for the same medium. There is no standardized handbook to interpret the symbols received in mediumship, but through practice, a medium develops his or her personal "dictionary" of symbolic meanings, whereby interpreting a message becomes a process of translating the symbols. It is clear why mediums get better with practice, because the medium's symbolic vocabulary grows as it would with exposure and experience in any new language. A flood of symbolic images can more easily be pieced together into a coherent message when one knows the vocabulary.

One medium at the Windbridge Institute noted that sometimes a discarnate spirit will show her two screens of information. If one side is "heavy" and the other softer and more ethereal, it indicates that what the discarnate believed in his or her physical life has changed and is no longer believed. Or it is now believed in a different way, as what is revealed in the afterlife apparently is different from what most traditional religions teach. The Windbridge Institute notes that discarnates who were very religious while alive on earth often are unwilling to "talk" about religion (Beischel, 2014). They do not espouse religion in their messages but use their earthly religious dedication only to identify themselves to loved ones. Not surprisingly, their perceptions have been etherealized and they probably no longer embrace the same limited religious beliefs they had while alive on earth.

Our breakdown of communication with the dead is that most of us have no idea how to do it. After all, it is a conversation from a sender and a receiver, and a communication breakdown can happen on either side. According to mediums, those of us in the body typically are on the receiving end of the conversation. The deceased person apparently can learn how to initiate a conversation with us, which is fortunate because we are stumbling in the dark about how to initiate a conversation with them. One researcher, the esoterically-named Dianne Arcangel (yes that is her real name), has a database of 10,000 after-death communications, and she notes that 88 percent of them arrived unexpectedly (Arcangel, 2005). This verifies that those of us in bodies are rarely the initiators of a conversation with someone who has passed on. Although it is perhaps unfortunate that we know so little about how and when to initiate communication from our side, this statistic diminishes a common objection that such communication is a hallucination taking root in badly wanting a message from a departed loved one.

It certainly seems that our departed loved ones want to communicate with us, but we are not attuned well enough to receive the messages. They may even be screaming at us from the other side and we are oblivious to it. Pam Grout has colorfully said that we "are accusing the higher force of not giving us clear guidance and we're the ones with our damned phones off the hook." (E-2, p. 95) This further explains why mediums and people attuned to receiving such messages are more likely to get messages for us than we are ourselves. Although fictional, this is theatrically displayed in the movie *Ghost*, where the Whoopi Goldberg character, Oda Mae Brown, serves as a messenger between lovers because she is the only one in the area who can hear the messages from Sam Wheat, the discarnate lover played by Patrick Swayze (Rubin, 1990). We should remember that messages can be symbolic and very subtle. Rather like psi, messages are more akin to a waft of wind presenting a diffused dreamlike symbol. Such messages are easily missed because we are accustomed to communicating physically and not via energy.

Nonetheless, we can hone our skills to become a better message antenna, but we should not expect to get perfect signal reception. Television is guilty of portraying mediumship with clear visual images, similar to a movie or YouTube video. Outside of symbolic mental communication, the discarnate may be able to use props in our environment to send us messages. We might encounter some meaningful movement of small objects or electrical manipulations, but if we expect a manifestation on the ceiling, we should be resigned to disappointment.

# CHAPTER

## 17

# APPARITIONS—DELIVERING
# A MESSAGE "IN PERSON"

As FOR MANIFESTATIONS ON THE ceiling, it is unlikely, but it could happen. Reports of apparitions are more common than one might expect, given the remnants of disbelief that permeate our culture. According to Oxford author Chris Carter, about one-fourth of the population has perceived the nearness of a deceased person and about three-fourths of these people had the experience more than once. Icelandic and British researchers noticed a statistical trend that apparitions occurred more often when the deceased person had died violently, amounting to about 30 percent of all apparitions (Carter, Science and the Afterlife Experience, 2012, p. 80). Researchers have some disagreements about how many apparitions are visual, but these are the easiest ones to study. John Palmer found that only 44 percent were visual in his Virginia research, Erlendur Haraldsson reported 67 percent in his Iceland study, and Celia Green and Charles McCreery found that 84 percent were visual (Green, 1975, p. 50). More than half happened in full light and interestingly, in rare cases when a mirror was available at the time of a visual apparition, the apparition was found to reflect in the mirror (Harraldson, 1994). Although most apparitions are seen by only one person, when two people are present at the time, Fred Myers determined that the apparition is seen by both people two-thirds of the time. In a separate study, Hornell Hart found that in 26 of 46 such cases (57 percent), the apparition was seen by both people (Myers & Stevenson, 1982) and (Hart, 1956).

There are three common theories about apparitions. Actually there are only two, since the first maintains that all apparitions are misperception, subjective hallucinations, or fraud, essentially saying that real apparitions do not exist. This is the easiest explanation to discard based on the empirical research mentioned above. The second is that apparitions of departed people are telepathic transfers of information, and the third is that visual apparitions are actual physical manifestations. Because apparitions are precise enough for witnesses to identify the person they saw in photographs, the third theory fits real experience the best.

Even more convincingly, when apparitions have appeared to more than one person at the same time, visual perspective is honored. That is, two people witnessing the apparition from different angles will see it in the same location but see different sides of it, depending on the individual location and perspective of each witness. Essentially, if the apparition appears between two witnesses, the witnesses will report seeing different sides of the apparition's "body". Because one witness might see the back side while one sees the front, this argues that the apparition is some type of physical or metaphysical presence rather than a collective hallucination. This also makes it unlikely that people are simply sharing a psychic connection, since it would entail adding dimensional perspective to whatever was psychically shared.

Curiously, apparitions usually are dressed in recognizable clothing. While perspective argues that apparitions are real manifestations rather than illusions, the appearance of clothing raises an objection from critics. They argue that clothes should not have their own ghosts, so bodily manifestations should not be clothed. Since apparitions are almost always clothed, they argue that apparitions are hallucinations or, at best, telepathic communication. If the apparition is the astral body of a deceased carnal body, it seems peculiar that people would perceive clothing on the body. The answer could very well be that whatever intelligence lies behind the apparition, it knows what it is doing. If the source is indeed a conscious entity from the spirit world and consciousness continues after death, this consciousness has not sacrificed its intelligence. An ability to appear at all requires intelligent conscious intent, so some faculty to utilize astral props consistent with that intent would be expected. For whatever purpose it has in mind, the apparition obviously wants to appear in a form that is identifiable. Apparitions do not appear in just any clothing but in something witnesses report as particularly identifiable with the person. The appearance of an apparition in characteristic clothing may be solely to be recognized. In response to the concern that clothing should not have its own morphogenetic field and ghost, Chris Carter notes that hair is not a living item either, so the materialization of clothing should pose no greater problem than the materialization of hair (Carter, Science and the Near-Death Experience: How Consciousness Survives Death, 2010, p. 89)

Clothing is basically a prop, and the use of other props for the sake of communication is very common in apparitions. The form of Owen Howerson, a soldier killed when his tank was hit in 1944, appeared to a relative, Georgina, asking her to tell his mother that he had been killed (Carter, Science and the Afterlife Experience, 2012, pp. 116-117) It is not clear why Owen chose Georgina to deliver this message, and because this point was bewildering to her, she asked the apparition for some proof. Owen's apparition plainly understood her request and drew a blue orchid out of his jacket with the words "Table Mountain". This made no sense to Georgina, but the image made perfect sense to Owen's mother, then living thousands of miles away in South Africa. Owen had once climbed Table Mountain there and picked a rare blue flower that only grew on that mountain. He had hidden the flower in is jacket and, on his return home, presented it to his mother. Because it had been illegal to pick this flower, only he and his mother knew about this event, making this a powerful way to authenticate the message. Both the jacket and the flower were clearly visible to Georgina in the apparition and served to convey information between the only two people on earth that would understand the message.

You may wonder why Owen's apparition chose to appear to Georgina rather than to Owen's mother himself. After all, the message was intended for Owen's mother. When apparitions choose to go through an intermediary, it is speculated that only certain people are open enough to the apparition's energy to perceive it. This could be the same reason that mediums are badgered to deliver messages to loved ones in the presence of the medium. For whatever reason—perhaps a lack of skill in this arena—the loved one is not able to perceive the communication directly.

My mother witnessed an apparition where clothing helped her identify the person. While employed as a nurse at the Memorial Hospital in El Campo, Texas, she had been assigned a patient named Merle. He was seriously ill and before he died, he asked my mother and another nurse to hold his hand because he "did not want to go alone", but he did pass on. Within a week thereafter, my mother turned a corner of a hospital wing and the figure of Merle stood there in the hallway. My mother firmly believes it was Merle partly because his very recognizable figure was clearly dressed in his distinctively pleated charcoal pants. After obviously appearing, his apparition simply disappeared. My mom did not get any message from this apparition, but clearly perceived his face. His clothing served as a distinct identifier. Perhaps Merle was simply acknowledging thanks and showing that he was not alone.

Apparitions by definition include the unexpected and unusual appearance of remarkable phenomena, so they need not be in human or animate form. But apparitions generally take human form because they usually communicate a message, and they differ from ghostly hauntings in that respect. Ghostly hauntings may be seen repeatedly in the same area and ghosts generally show little awareness of their current surroundings. In fact, a European monastery had been rebuilt in the 1700s and dirt was excavated, so that the floor of the newer monastery was lowered about three feet. Ghostly monks are repeatedly seen walking on their old floor, hovering about three feet above the current floor, oblivious to the change that was made after their time on earth. Ghostly hauntings often perform such repetitive actions, like replaying a movie over and over, and consequently appear to be nothing more than remnant energy fields. True human apparitions, on the other hand, maintain personality characteristics and are recognizable as a particular person.

As with OBEs and NDEs, the most convincing evidence for consciousness survival comes when an apparition of a departed soul delivers messages that are surprising and could not otherwise be known, but nonetheless turn out to be true. The James Chaffin case is an excellent example of a discarnate message that delivered information no one knew. This report is from Chris Carter's excellent study of science and the afterlife (Carter, Science and the Afterlife Experience, 2012, pp. 120-124). Chaffin was a North Carolina farmer in the early twentieth century. After his death, his apparition vividly visited his son in a state between waking and sleeping, to relay the message that his most recent will and testament was in an overcoat pocket which had been sewn shut. On finding the overcoat and cutting open the pocket, there was merely a message in James' handwriting that said to read the 27th chapter of Genesis in his own father's old Bible. In the pages of this chapter, which is the Genesis story of Jacob winning his birthright from Esau, the family found a more recent will than the one they had used to distribute James Chaffin's estate. In the older will, James had left nothing to his widow and three sons, but his more recent will wanted them included. Interviews in a subsequent probate found that no one was aware that James had written a newer will, which is why no one had opposed the previous will. Ten witnesses swore that the later will found in the Bible was made in James Chaffin's handwriting.

Apparitions that deliver messages are especially convincing when the apparition is communal, an occasional occurrence where more than one person witnesses the same apparition. Sometimes, such apparitions are accompanied by other unexplained phenomena, such as the Miracle of the Sun during the apparition of the mother of Jesus at the Cova da Iria in Fatima, Portugal, an event witnessed by more than 30,000 people (Miracle of the Sun, 2015). Although research indicates that only about one out of eight apparitions is witnessed by more than one person, the proportion fits the time people spend alone. In other words, the main reason that most apparitions are witnessed by only one person is that the person witnessing it is alone at the time it occurs.

Apparitions, in most cases, are a convincing method for delivering a message. Manifestations that look physical, with props like clothing, help a discarnate spirit get messages across more clearly, essentially using the apparitional form as a tool or vehicle for delivering a message in a persuasive way. These may be the classiest conduits for message delivery from the other side. With an apparition, there is no need for the discarnate spirit to employ a medium!

CHAPTER

# 18

# KEEPING OUR AFTERLIFE
# TELEPHONES ON THE HOOK

IF YOU WANT A MESSAGE from a departed loved one, wanting it too badly may actually block your ability to perceive it, even if it is given. If you doggedly work to capture a butterfly, it will elude you, but if you let go, you might just find it landing on your shoulder. Grief can produce overwhelming emotions that make us unable to pick up subtle messages. Perhaps the discarnate loved one is aware that you are not yet ready to receive a message. Sometimes people are angry with God and consequently turn off their receivers. Ironically, some people really want a message but are afraid of a "haunting", so fear itself can veto the sending and receiving of a message.

Let's give our departed loved ones the benefit of the doubt if they do not send us obvious messages. We have looked at the many roadblocks to communication between us and those we call the dead. One, manifesting themselves to our senses is not simple for someone without a physical body. There is indeed the great gulf or chasm spoken about in Luke 2:16 between those of us still in our bodies and those who have passed to the other side. Our physical eyes can only pick up stimuli grounded in physical matter, but our departed loved ones are no longer physical. All the ways that we have learned to communicate with each other are no longer there when a person leaves the body. Because our discarnate loved ones no longer have physical bodies that can touch ours, even when there is communication, we do not know how to listen and may actually have our receivers turned off. On top of that, the messages we get from those that have passed will are usually symbolic, and something is lost in the colossal task of translating symbolic messages. As though that is not enough, we have noted that time is different for us and for them, so what is a long time for us body dwellers is an instant for them. Finally, there is knowledge we should not know in order for us to make the most of our earthly incarnation, a kind of divine prime directive that allows only certain messages to get through.

A strong piece of advice for someone who wants to be contacted by a loved one who has died is to eliminate any doubt that communication is possible, and then relax and be open (Dillard, 2013). It is best just to be patient and remember that requesting an intercession through prayer cannot hurt. Then remain receptive and even ask out loud to be contacted, but recognize that we are not at the controls. Messages are likely to be more subtle and unconvincing than we would like, so do not expect a manifestation on the ceiling. One medium at the Windbridge Institute suggests that we look for fireflies rather than fireworks. Remain disciplined, not letting your imagination trick you. If it the message is real, it may be subtle, but it will be persistent.

# ◼ Closing Remarks on the Afterlife

I realize that the topic of afterlife communication may still sound farfetched to some of us, but if you have read this far, you are at least open minded about it. As for me, I genuinely believe that

# PART IV
## REAPING THE PSYCHIC HARVEST

CHAPTER

# 19

# PSYCHIC MESSAGES COMING HOME

THE FOCUS OF THIS BOOK now shifts to a fun part for me, and I hope it is for you. We have looked at some scientific evidence for the intentional creation of the universe, for the existence of psi, and for consciousness survival after death. Now it is time to harvest the benefits of the search. You may remain unconvinced about the reality of psi and the survival of consciousness, but I fully expect mounting evidence to continue expanding over time. If you are a doubter, I ask you to suspend your disbelief temporarily and join me in some personal stories, including messages I have received in meditation and prayer. I have already shared some personal psychic stories in the context of the research evidence, but this part will be less formal, more like stories around a campfire. As humans, our personal lived experiences touch us emotionally more than scientific research results, but I still think statistically, so the reality of personal psychic revelations is enhanced for me the more unlikely they are. Nonetheless, my beliefs remain tinged as much by subjective revelations and anecdotal experiences as by evidence,

I find that messages encountered psychically or in meditation have given me valuable insights that make life richer and more understandable. I am grateful for the "wow" moments that have convinced me more than scientific discoveries, which admittedly remain far from complete. Those who are certain that the paranormal is hokum probably threw this book aside long before getting to this page (if they ever even read a word of it). But since you are still reading, I thank you for your open-mindedness and tolerance for my writing style. I hope I am able to share meaningful information and perhaps convey an insight or two.

It is a bit awkward shifting from an insistence on evidence to sharing my own revelations, since I have endeavored to retain an evidence-based perspective so far. That is less the result of any doubt on my part than it is an attempt to convince doubtful readers that much paranormal weirdness is not accidental and coincidental, but purposeful. Proof is not a goal that will be achieved here, but there is no point in letting the fruit of a psychic harvest rot because it does not look ripe.

We all experience inexplicable events that crop into our lives, but the benefit of being the author is that one "gets the floor". I certainly would love to hear your experiences and revelations and invite you to share them with me and those that read this book. (You may contact me at Gary Preuss on Facebook or via my e-mail address for this book, which is *austinowl@aol.com*.) My literature research indicates that psi, revelations, and messages from the dead are available to everyone, and the evidential signs are that they are purposeful. These messages are part of what inspired—and even goaded—me to write this book. That goading inspiration, I believe, is also evidence of psi and intention, the way that divinity asks us to fulfill a destiny. If we ignore the inspiration, it pushes harder, intent on eliciting our response. Acting on it is to be *in spirit*, meaning that our response to inspiration brings us in union with the divine.

I was taught about God as a child, so I was predisposed to see what looks like magic in everyday life. But I was also brought up in a very practical, down-to-earth way, so I was taken aback by those unexpected psychic experiences in the extracurricular Silva Mind

Control classes. I was disheartened that the walls of bias did not crumble in the face of accurate psychic experiences that are highly improbable but nonetheless happening. I realize that everyone's experiences are different, so those with reliable psychic encounters would believe in the phenomena more than those without them. For me, the psychic events I already have shared convinced me that what feels like imagination at first can be a real source of information. But reality is so weird that it often feels unreal, and Johann Wolfgang von Goethe once suggested that "Few people have the imagination for reality" (Goethe, 1749-1832). So stay awhile longer, as we explore revelations that I have been thankful to receive in meditation, prayer, and simply following the drifts of intuition day-to-day.

## ■ Tuning in to Past Life Memories

Here is a past life memory that unfolded with some startling new evidence of its own. I have a strong affinity for desert mountain landscapes and feel very much at home in them, even though I grew up in a humid Gulf coast climate. The colors and patterns of Southwestern U.S. Indian art find their way into my clothing and house décor, particularly that of the Anasazi Indians, although the Anasazi name was not how this tribe referred to itself. (I discovered that they were labeled "Anasazi" by their adversaries.) Frequently in meditations, I had "memories" as a young hunter, and although I was part of a Native American community, my memories usually recall times when I was alone. I had always just assumed these were imaginings. Given my penchant for spiritual information, one night I prayed in a meditation to understand why these imaginings kept coming back. I asked if these memories were grounded in a physical place and, if so, that I be given information to locate that place.

My answer was an immediate image of the word "Winchester", and the mental image in my mind was the current state of Arizona. The name Winchester, however, seemed ridiculous to me. Although Winchester has some association with the American Southwest because of the Winchester rifle, it certainly is not an American Indian name or reference. I got a subsequent revelation that Winchester is not what the region was called during the time of my memory, but a means for me to locate the area on a map. That made sense, so I started a search for Winchester, Arizona—and, disappointingly, found nothing. At the time, which was many years ago, I was using physical maps, but as Internet mapping capabilities provided more research opportunities, I discovered that there is a Winchester mountain range in the southeastern deserts of Arizona, in the sparsely settled area midway between Tucson and the border of New Mexico.

At first this seemed to be my answer, since my apparent past life memories included desert mountains, but there was a fatal flaw in this geography. If my memories were from an Anasazi tribe, the location was wrong, since historians had recorded that the Anasazi lived much farther north, concentrated mostly around the Four Corners region where Colorado, Utah, Arizona, and New Mexico come together. The closest known Anasazi settlement was about two hundred miles north of the Winchester Mountains. Maybe my identification with Anasazi art and customs was, once again, just a preference, with no previous-life connection.

About seven or eight years ago, I was browsing through my morning newspaper and felt a strong tingling in my spine when I noticed a small headline about the discovery of an Anasazi settlement far from where the Anasazi were known to have lived. This location was about two hundred miles south of the southernmost settlement previously known to have existed, in southeastern Arizona. The article went on to speculate on how and when the Anasazi could have settled here and on how much farther afield their settlements might have gone. The Winchester Mountains are quite remote and located largely on private land today, and I have discovered no paved public roads to get into them, but I suspect I might recognize particular locations if I ever have the chance to wander through them.

Children who remember past lives, particularly when their stories are verified by external sources, present us with an intriguing bit of evidence for the survival of consciousness. In fact, Carl Sagan argued that past life experiences were evidence for the reality of psi. Dr. Ian Stevenson has extensively researched this phenomenon and published stories of mostly Asian children who remembered people and places that were never part of their present lives. Jim Tucker, a psychiatrist and professor of neurobehavioral sciences studied mostly American children and proposed a theory of reincarnation consistent with quantum mechanics. Separated by distance and time and completely different relatives, the children could not have known what they knew, unless one allowed for memories from a previous existence.

When these memories are verified as true, we are back to explaining something extra normal. The subject of Raymond Moody's classic book on near-death experiences, *Life After Life*, was cleverly echoed in Jim Tucker's *Life Before Life*, where the focus is on children remembering previous incarnations. Dr. Tucker, a child psychologist, conducted research at the University of Virginia's Division of Perceptual Studies and has encountered children whose memories of a previous existence extend so far that they can identify the names of people they have never met in old photographs that they have never seen (Tucker & Stevenson, 2008).

# ▪ An Intuitive Stomach

I have noted that intuition usually is quite gentle, leading us to wonder whether it is just coincidental when something needles at us. But on rare occasions, it can be frantically insistent. When faced with a choice, we know that intuition can urge us in one direction or another and we may even welcome the guidance. Sometimes it stubbornly insists on taking us where we do not want to go.

Most of my intuitive "hits" are mental, taking the form of thoughts. A few are emotional, such as sudden urgings that color one's feelings, making something seem particularly attractive or repellant. But some psychic intuition is physical, to the degree that some physical ailments disappear when a person leaves a bad job or relationship. There are numerous accounts of people who failed to board an airline that crashed or who missed being at 9-11 worksites on the day of the tragedy, with rates of sickness significantly higher on such occasions than on a typical day. Consider that some of the choir members who were impeded from going to their Nebraska church on the night that it blew up were faced with odd physical problems that night.

Such was the case when I was invited to a club potluck Christmas party and gift exchange on the evening of December 12, 2009. I was looking forward to going, and on the basis of my house address, the party host asked that I bring a salad or an appetizer. So I was preparing a huge fruit salad concoction, slicing up a dozen different fancy fruits to be topped with cherries and coconut. It was about two hours before I planned to leave for the party, and in snacking on some of the fruits as I sliced them, I started to feel sick at my stomach. Still, I finished preparing the big bowl of fruit salad, and took my dachshund, Daisy, on her daily long walk. My stomach was getting increasingly unsettled. It was a Saturday and I had spent a few hours in climbing around the house doing electrical repairs earlier in the day, so decided I might just be tired or hungry, but I now had a serious stomach ache. After getting back from walking Daisy, I decided to lie down, but the pain had grown too strong for resting or sleeping. The sickness was isolated to my stomach so I thought it might be food poisoning, but about the only thing I had eaten that day was the fruit I had been snacking on while preparing the salad. Was this appendicitis or something worse?

I remembered that heat often sooths muscle spasms. Since I have a hot tub that is kept heated during the colder months, I decided to go soak in the spa's hot water. The pain in my stomach was growing more intense, and to make things worse, poor Daisy insisted on shivering next to the hot tub while I was in it. It was a foggy, dreary, and particularly cold evening for Austin, Texas. I hated to see Daisy shiver, so to reduce the suffering of at least one of us (Daisy's), I went indoors to sit in a tub of hot bath water instead.

This hot water cure did not work, so my thoughts turned to seeking medical assistance, but I decided first to employ a psychic healing method I had been studying in the coursework at the American Institute of Holistic Theology. Despite the pain, I forced myself to begin a simple healing meditation.

As can happen with psi, I got more results than I expected.

The unusual feature about this particular meditation message was that it was absolutely clear and insistent, unlike so much spirit guidance that is muted and easily dismissed as imagination. I was told very distinctly that the stomach pain was a patent message that I should not go to the potluck party.

I was concerned about the pain but I still yearned not to miss this Christmas potluck and party, but this message was absolutely determined to get my attention. So I mentally agreed not to go the potluck party, and quite remarkably for someone who still has a hard time trusting the "woo-woo" element of an intuitive hit, the pain dissipated almost completely. This had been a disconcerting pain, as the next step on my agenda was to seek emergency health care, but now the persistent pain was very suddenly gone, immediately sliding away at the moment I decided not to go the party. Even though I had learned not to be surprised by following an intuitive hit, I found this sudden disappearance of severe pain hard to believe. I did not go to the potluck party, and the pain did not show up again.

Even after many years of prayer and dabbling in psychic phenomena, such events still amaze me and make me a bit unsettled, in case it reflects a problem with my psychological or physical health. As soon as the pain suddenly left, I knew that this was a clear psychic message, but now I had a new concern, which was a really huge bowl of potentially tainted fruit salad. After all, I had been snacking on the fruit while preparing the salad and this might have been some peculiar food poisoning, despite the remarkably sudden subsidence of pain. I was still meditating when this thought hit, so I asked for guidance about the fruit salad—simply asking whether it was OK to eat. I did not relish the thought of tossing out a huge expensive creation of rather exotic winter fruit salad on the suspicion that it might be tainted. Given the pain I had endured, I wondered if the papaya I had put in it (which had been suspiciously cheap, rather mushy, and a bit unusual in taste) was at the root of my sickness. When I asked whether the fruit salad was safe to eat, again I got a definite answer, which was yes. Even in meditation, I can be rather headstrong and had no desire to risk a repeat of this searing sickness by eating tainted food. Suspicious about this answer, I asked again, and I received an image of my primary spirit guide patting me on the back with a "tut-tut", and telling me again with a determined "believe it this time!" that the fruit salad had nothing wrong with it. I was told that the pain had been a message put there *solely* to keep me from going to the potluck.

With a bit of "psychic tester" doubt, I ate some of the fruit salad over the next day. When there was no bad reaction, I eventually shared and finished the remainder. It tasted good, and I had no negative physical reactions from eating it. This event was meaningful enough for me to share it with the professional staff at the American Institute of Holistic Theology, included as an example of intuitive hits that present themselves physically. To have stomach cramps akin to severe food poisoning and have the symptoms disappear suddenly when I agreed not to go to the potluck party could be an

# CHAPTER

## 20

# THE ROAD NOT TAKEN— AN ACT OF FAITH

WHEN WE MAKE A CHOICE between two alternatives in most of our daily decisions, we seldom know what would have happened had we taken the other option. Research on the value of following intuition faces this dilemma. When we use intuitive hits to follow a particular path, we simply do not know what would have happened if we had ignored the intuition or responded to the intuitive nudge in a different way. So how can we measure which was the better option? When we are confronted with a decision and intuition prods (or shoves) us to choose between alternatives, we know the results of the choice we made. If I am on a road trip and reach an intersection with a choice between taking two equally possible alternatives and I get a hunch that one way is preferable, I usually follow that hunch. At the end of the trip, if nothing seems especially rewarding about the choice I made, it seems that the intuitive hit was nothing more than an imaginative whim. Still, would I have encountered something unpleasant had I taken the other route? I do not know. Sometimes news reports might give me an answer, such as a reported traffic slowdown or accident on the road not taken, but usually there is no news either way. Mostly life gives us little or no validation for our choice.

In the flight example, we occasionally read the stories of people who followed their intuition and avoided taking a flight that was seriously delayed or crashed. These are impressive, but what about the undoubtedly countless times when people get an intuitive feeling not to board a flight, but the flight completed its route uneventfully? Were these intuitive errors? Maybe yes, but maybe no. With all the permutations in life, maybe the intuition was related to something else about taking the trip at that time, not just the flight itself. The flight may have been fine, but some other aspect of the trip may be a mistake. What happens to us is related to where we will be at a precise point in time, with each choice leaving us in different places at different times. In walking along a street or driving on a road, arriving one second earlier or later can be the difference between a close call and a fatal accident. A delay may be all that is necessary to alter one's experience markedly. Research on the efficacy of intuitive hits is a slippery endeavor, since it is not possible to isolate all the permutations and combinations of life. So determining whether a psychic hit was "correct" remains mostly a matter of faith, sourced in appreciation for the times that we were thankful for following the obviously positive ones.

So regardless of the difficulty with getting hard data on the value of psychic intuition, what is important in our lives is how we can benefit from trusting an intuitive message. One advantage to such intuitive guidance is that we can ask for another intuitive message to answer why choosing one vector is better than another. While I was still in the healing meditation when my stomach pain suddenly disappeared, I did exactly that. You may not know what would have happened had you ignored your intuition, but you can ask.

Remember that psychic impressions are gifts, and wisdom says we will not always get the gift we want. During that meditation when I was distinctly told not to attend the Christmas potluck, I asked why, and I received a straightforward and direct message that it was not for me to know yet. The feisty part of me was saying, "Really? You're using pain to push me into a decision and you give me a non-answer from some corny psychic television program?" A generic and nonspecific "It's not for you to know" did not sit well with my inquiring mind. Since I was now feeling so much better and fascinated by the obvious message I got, I stubbornly pursued a more precise answer, and received another distinct answer that I "had to be available to perform a task". Another hackneyed answer, but at least this was a bit more specific. Still, this blunt answer made it clear that I was not in a position to bargain for more information. Since I have received very loving messages from God-given spirit guides in past meditations, I have grown to trust them in the faith that I would be told all that I needed to know. But given the strong direct message and the quick release of pain when I decided to stay home on the night of the Christmas party, I still wonder what specifically would have happened had I ventured out to the party that night. The strong intuitive demand in this case probably gave me no choice. That is, had I remained determined to go to the party, I suspect that my pain would not have subsided, so I would have been kept away from the party by default. I never asked about the task I was to perform by not venturing out that night.

Judging whether an intuitive hit is accurate becomes a subjective guess. Intuition does not easily lend itself to scientific study because intuitive hunches cannot be called up on demand and because the massive number of possibilities in life presents a roadblock for determining whether one choice is better than another. Since the underlying cause of intuition is not understood, anecdotal evidence is all we really have. The late Dr. David R. Hawkins was convinced that the reason intuition cannot be measured scientifically is because it lies in the spiritual dimension (Hawkins D. R., 2005), and science is a measuring stick that cannot be applied in the realm of the spiritual. I emphasize this point again because, if it is true, we may never get a scientific handle on the mechanisms that make intuition work.

Still, there are patterns in circumstantial stories that increase our understanding of intuition and give us potentially useful information. One such curious pattern is that successful psychics often have survived life-threatening events, where their psychic and intuitive abilities either began or improved dramatically after these serious events. The internet has many stories of psychic and intuitive abilities that are heightened after some tragedy, and I found a 2015 website dedicated to this topic at *http://www.psychic-experiences.com/real-psychic-story.php?story=5047.* Many published psychics, healers, and medical intuitives have mentioned such life-changing turning points in their lives. Judith Orloff and John Holland both had brushes with death in traffic accidents and David Hawkins nearly died of exposure in a snowstorm as a child, a *metanoia* moment for him. These events awakened, reawakened, or enhanced the intuitive strengths of these noted luminaries.

Is a very determined intuitive hit more likely to be correct than a subtle psychic whisper? Subjectively, the answer is yes, but determined intuitive messages may still turn out to be wrong. It could be the right choice at one time, but it may be surprising to learn that intuition can "change its mind". Our intuitive sense does not have all its information at once, particularly if grounded in the hypersensitivity proposed by Nancy de Tertre, so communication we receive psychically is subject to updates.

One of the best examples of this was shared by Sonia Choquette in one of her audio programs, where she relayed an experience in shopping for a house (Choquette, Your Psychic Pathway: Listening to the Guiding Wisdom of your Soul, 1993). Sonia saw a perfect house that immediately attracted her, so she practically railroaded her reluctant husband to agree to the purchase. After a sale contract was drawn up, Sonia's intuition made a 180-degree turn. She did not know why, but suddenly she felt compelled not to buy the house. Her husband told her that she had pressed their commitment to buy, so if she now felt differently, she had to get them out. Without really knowing why, other than trusting her all-encompassing compulsion not to buy a house that had so dreamily attracted her earlier, she managed to disengage them from the contract. A few weeks later she found out why her intuition had pushed her so strongly in an opposite direction. The house of her dreams had been severely damaged in a flood, losing nearly all its value. If there is a lesson here, it is that intuitive impulses can be wrong and be updated with new information, so it is one paranormal arena where time appears to be a factor. Perhaps more likely, Sonia simply failed to employ her intuitive guidance in her initial attraction to the house.

# ■ Dodging Regret: Avoiding *"Shouda"* and *"Couda"*

I am guilty of the latter problem, which is not requesting intuitive guidance when it might be helpful. Intuition can guide us into good luck and guide us out of bad luck events, but the strength of the message varies, and we may not be aware enough for it to hit us over the head in an obvious way. If the feeling is mild, we might miss acting on it, only to think back to a "should have" moment that we overlooked. Such failings could be an invitation to grow that requires some deep internal work. On the occasion of my stomach pain that receded, had I not done some psychic work in my doctoral training, I would not have done the meditation that gave me the message not to go to the party. Without the tools of this training, I may have stubbornly plowed ahead until my stomach pain forced me to stay home or seek emergency health care. Such costly circumstances can force their way into our lives if we do not use the psychic tools at our disposal, while taking the psychic route may make the road less expensive and much easier. It may take years to discover and work through these lessons, as in the following example from my life dating way back to college.

My upbringing included fatherly guidance that being physically strong and not lazy was a virtue, so I have always been somewhat of a closet athlete. My father had been a decorated war veteran who inculcated in my brother and me that hard physical work was a virtue in itself. I remember him remarking that if we needed to miss church on a Holy Day because inclement weather forced us to bale hay immediately, that work itself was prayer. So I was in excellent physical shape when I started college, having spent most of the previous summer working in hay fields with my dad. My summer had included hauling and stacking thousands of heavy hay bales onto trailers and into hot sweaty barns on the humid Texas coast. I was in excellent physical shape when I started my freshman year at Rice University, so when the physical education department tested us for speed and endurance, I performed so well that I was assigned to the top-tier physical education class for non-scholarship athletes.

At the end of the fall semester, we were physically tested again, and although I had excellent grades in my academic courses, I was given Rice's equivalent of a "C" in my physical education class.

This did not sit well with me, since my bias about being physically strong made me worry that someone who saw that grade on my record would think I was an academic scholar but a physical weakling. On top of that, some of my friends who mostly ignored their physical fitness received better grades in physical education than me. I asked the department why I got the "C" and was told that it was the highest grade given to anyone who performed worse on the physical tests at the end of the semester than at the beginning. If a student was not in better shape at the end of the semester than at the beginning, this indicated that he or she was not dedicated to the physical education the course offered. Not accessing my intuition at the time, how was I to have known this? It was no surprise that my physical shape eroded after a semester of long hours of sedentary study, compared to the physical rigor of the previous summer. Philosophically, I admitted that I had indeed put less emphasis on my physical education than my academic classes, but I still had the second semester to play by their rules and get the grade I wanted on my record.

For the second semester, I had a different physical education professor. Great, here was my chance to have my physical education grade come up to the standards of my academic grades. I made sure the professor knew that I was motivated. Yet again, I was not using my intuition, and as fate might have it, this professor passed away suddenly right before the spring semester ended. When the grades came out, I got another "C" in physical education. I was mortified and immediately requested why I got a "C" this time, and I was told that the professor had not submitted grades before his unexpected death, and without them, the department decided to give everyone the same grade received in the first semester. That seemed wrong and ridiculous, but the sudden death of my professor made it seem insensitive to make an issue of something fundamentally trivial while everyone was dealing with the death of a colleague. But it subsequently irked me over the years that, indeed, my Rice transcript would appear that I was an academic nerd making excellent grades in everything but physical education. And it would be on my transcript through history, even to someone who dug it out a hundred years later.

But this episode had its benefits, including teaching me lessons to follow my intuition about the course of action to take to avoid unfortunate events. I can see now that it was a small lesson that provided opportunities. In fact, a couple of years after graduation, during a professional job interview, my interviewer and prospective supervisor noted those grades in physical education during my freshman year and asked me about them. This provided me a chance to relay the story you just read, and the supervisor was impressed with my ability to make a positive argument out of a negative circumstance, so it helped me get a good research job at the nation's United Way of America headquarters in Alexandria,

Virginia. Also, those physical education grades helped keep me healthier throughout my life, as I psychologically chose many behaviors to keep my physical body healthier than a "C" specimen. I spent my entire working career commuting to work by bicycle, and my life as a bicycle commuter was grounded as much in this attitude as it was in environmental convictions. And now I have a chance to share in writing my take on something that has needled me a bit for years. For anyone who might care enough to snoop through my college transcript 100 years from now, you have my explanation in writing!

Intuition may not be given when there is a life lesson that must be learned. I had ample opportunities to intuit positive responses in my college physical education course, but this was before I was aware that intuition could be usefully tapped. Also, if this situation was a life lesson I was supposed to endure, it would not have mattered anyway. As noted before, the gift of psi is not intended to protect us from life's often harsh lessons, but it can help us to help others. Our emotions are instigators of many intuitive urgings that drive us to take action, maybe to drop outmoded beliefs that are more damaging than useful. Events invite us to look at our beliefs and clear away ancient decisions that are not supporting us. In his book, *I Can See Clearly Now*, Wayne Dyer relays events in his personal history that had to happen for him to grow in ways necessary to fulfill the purposes of his life. Our history unfolds as it does for reasons that may not be clear at the time, but eventually reveal themselves if we honestly look at them. What looks negative at one time can reveal a positive silver lining later.

I was hurt badly by the sudden death of my friend, David Austin, but his death had an unexpected impact on me, as I am sure it did for many others. Timed as it was, this tragic event, closed a door for me, but it was a career change that I was not comfortable taking. It has freed me with the time and opportunity to work on alternatives that inspired me, such as writing this book. I have no desire or intention to underplay his death, but negative setbacks in one area often present opportunities for miracles in another. Besides, as you probably have guessed, I believe in the evidence that our physical deaths are nothing more than starting a new life chapter anyway.

> When the Lord closes a door, somewhere He opens a window.
>
> 
> --The Sound of Music<br>
> (Julie Andrews' script for the character<br>
> of Maria von Trapp) (Wise, 1965)
> 

CHAPTER

# 21

# HARNESSING OUR
# MIRACULOUS ABILITIES

WHEN I THINK ABOUT MIRACLES, Jesus Christ usually comes to mind as
a true avatar. He exemplified a philosophy of life that has passed
the truth test through the ages. Divinity may be the reason for
his miraculous powers, but anyone dedicated to his lifestyle and
teachings would naturally share his ability to perform miracles.
Miracles are not unusual throughout history. Many people believe
that Sathya Sai Baba, the late Indian spiritual leader, and present
day healers such as the Brazilian John of God have showered us with
these truly paranormal phenomena. The skeptic might say that there
is no proof that Christ performed miracles or that he even existed,
but Christian and Roman texts indicate that he drew crowds among
a largely uneducated populace in a time without social networks
and mass communication. Something about him was so appealing
and persuasive that word-of-mouth stories made people flock to
see him, and the signs Christ performed are noted as a reason he
was so well known to the political leaders of the time. Even though
his miracles were completely altruistic, they ironically made him so
threatening to the authorities that they managed to have him killed.

I bring up this great miracle worker to emphasize something he himself said about talents and capacities that we all have. We may be tempted to take the easy road and say that Christ's divinity greatly surpassed our own, so we cannot hope to perform the miracles he did. But I am intrigued that Christ himself played down a claim to special divinity, with remarks such as "It is you who say it". The Wisdom tradition argues that Christ was imparting an important message to us, which is that we *all* share his abilities. This message is captured scripturally in the tenth chapter of John, when Jesus Christ emphasizes that we all "are gods". This is extended in the fourteenth chapter of the same gospel, when Christ says that we all have the capacity "to do even greater things" than the miracles he performed on earth.

In the gnostic Gospel of Thomas, Christ says that combining thought and emotion together in peace literally gives us the power to move mountains. This was not metaphorical, but recorded precisely as an actual power within us. In fact, asking for something in prayer meant something different in the language Christ spoke on earth. The word "ask" in Aramaic translates directly into English as "claim" or "demand" (Grout, p. 82), so asking for something in prayer was making a powerful demand. Christ knew that he could do so. Likewise, St. Francis of Assisi said that "there are beautiful and wild forces within us," and believing this, he harnessed these forces to perform miracles of his own.

These are reminders that we are special and that miraculous abilities are within our grasp. The obvious question becomes why so few of us actually see such miracles in our lives. The difference between miracle workers and the rest of us may be that miracle workers are aware of—and awaken—the mostly dormant powers we all have. Sathya Sai Baba marveled many people in recent times with his miracles, to the point that an awed follower once asked him if he was God. Sai Baba reportedly said yes, which may seem presumptuous, but he followed this by saying, "So are you, and the only difference between you and me is that I know it and you doubt it." (Dyer, 2012) We are all connected to and share in the divine source, but in order to tap into the powers it provides, we need to believe it—really. Our innate dormant powers are captured in the clever title *You'll See it When You Believe It*, a compendium of Wayne Dyer's take on the powers we possess if we get our egos out of the way and really believe that we have these seemingly miraculous powers (Dyer, You'll See It When You Believe It, 1989).

Indeed, miracles related to psychic guidance show up in our lives when we know they are not unusual, when we let go of societal beliefs that they can only happen in mystical and rarefied places and times. I believe that miracle workers can perform miracles because they know they can command them, without any doubt. Yes, asking in prayer is indeed demanding an outcome.

The lack of doubt is absolutely fundamental and key. This power that comes from believing without doubt is displayed in another Christian story recorded in the gospel of Matthew (14th chapter), when Jesus walked on water in the Sea of Galilee. Once again we may be inclined to chalk this up to Christ being special and more than human. But I believe the real crux of the story for us is what happened next, to the very human apostle Peter. Seeing that it was Jesus on the water, Peter asked that Christ command him to walk on water too. When Christ said "Come", the gospel says that "Peter got out of the boat and *began to walk on the water* toward Jesus." Here was an ordinary flesh and blood human walking on water! The Christian gospel says it was only after Peter's doubts told him that he was doing something impossible that he became frightened and began to sink. If the story is physically accurate, there is a huge clue here that our seemingly insurmountable difficulty to produce miracles in our lives takes root in our inability to remain steadfast without doubt.

That is a difficult state to achieve within our "monkey minds" which are always ruminating about what can and cannot be done.

It certainly is a problem for me. Doubt underlies my psychic impressions, as I always ask myself if they are just imagination. Are they really real? If so, which ones? My next obstacle is my ego. There is a temptation to take credit for being psychic and believing that psychic abilities can be controlled by the ego. When the ego steps in, psi steps out.

Fortunately, we do not need to be responsible for the miracles to believe that we can command them. It is a delicate balancing act to believe steadfastly that what we ask for will be delivered while not believing that we are doing it ourselves. Totally getting the ego out of the way is a colossal challenge, and I suspect it is the dominant reason why most of us have such a poor track record at bringing about miracles. Doubt and ego keep my ability to harness God's psychic gifts in a state of arrested development.

I should know better, especially after discovering that my most accurate psychic impressions arise when I have not asked for them. Repeatedly, psychic hits that simply show up unannounced have accurate information. However, if I ask for them, I find that their accuracy is much more questionable. For a rather frivolous but telling example, I sometimes get a quick unrequested psychic impression of who will win a close football game that I am watching. I find that these spontaneous impressions are reliably accurate, even when a major turnaround in an early score may be necessary for this team to win. However, if I am watching such a game and consciously ask to know psychically who will win, the impressions I get are wrong as often as they are right. In my life, and I suspect for others, the impressions that are correct are gifts that show up unannounced, but attempts to control these gifts get the ego involved and the accuracy dissolves.

This presents a bit of a dilemma. What use are psychic abilities that are only reliably accurate when one cannot control them? How was Christ able to demand miracles? The answer appears to lie in that subtle balancing act with the ego. I believe it is by design that the power of psi dissolves when one is tempted to take credit for it. Because psychic abilities are intended to be altruistic, while seeking adulation for helping someone is not, the psychic energy disappears when our intention is self-serving. Remember what the psychic teacher Jose Silva uncovered about trying to use these abilities for personal gain or the evidence we looked at for picking lottery numbers psychically. Whatever psychic energy is, it is strongest when used purely to help others. It truly is a case of letting go and letting God, of being thankful when a psychic impression falls in one's lap and advises a course of action.

As such, it is a subtle balancing act when one is asking for psychic guidance, as the accuracy of an intuitive impression is related to one's reason for asking. I am not saying that one should not ask for insight. Just know that insights that arrive on one's doorstep unannounced are reliably accurate, while it is difficult to keep one's ego at bay when we ask for psychic information. More research on this may help us understand this tendency more fully. But it is certainly true in my life and it fits with the theory that psychic gifts are intended for positive purposes while not precluding us from learning life's lessons. Psychic impressions can help us guide others away from stepping in doggie doo, but their purpose is not to keep doggie doo off our own shoes.

## ■ About as Healthy as We Decide to Be

Traditional religions may indicate that health is in the hands of God, but we should take some responsibility for it. Whatever happens to us physically should be borne with acceptance but not resignation, because we have a right to heal. Our ego-based theories about God can be rather negative at times, so much so that the Christian scriptures show that Jesus Christ lived in a society that viewed physical illness as a punishment. Many still believe that God punishes us physically for offenses, such as crippling us with poor health, but such a vengeful god appears to be an ego-based god of our own creation.

In this light, it strikes me as strange that we imagine ourselves capable of making the Creator of everything happy or sad by our behavior. The Catholic prayer of contrition teaches us to say that "I am heartily sorry for having offended Thee", but a belief that we can offend the creator of the universe by our actions is a presumption that seems a bit silly. I do not want to belittle the value of contrition, but the assumption that we can offend a vengeful God is bizarre. If we are having physical problems, it is not because we are being punished, and Christ himself said that (Gospel of John, Chapter 9:3). Instead of believing in a punishing God, we should be confident to believe in a God that has provided us with innate healing powers.

Psychic information is useful for our conscious ability to heal, yet for too long, science has shied away from research on nontraditional methods of healing, including vibrational medicine and energy healing. I myself still harbor a culturally ingrained mindset that doubts my dachshund is displaying bona fide psychic ability, even when that seems the most straightforward explanation for her behaviors. Similar doubts prevent us from experiencing more health miracles in our lives, particularly regarding our intuitive ability to heal ourselves and others. Our culture still emphasizes that the way to tackle a health issue is to get a medical prescription or surgery, conveying that the only reliable way to heal something physical is to take or do something physical. Yes, medicine, surgeries, and physical therapy do have a proven track record that should not be ignored in healing the body, but as effective as this approach is, it is nonetheless incomplete.

Fortunately, medicine is gradually opening its doors to research the nontraditional. It has acknowledged the power of prayer through research, but even with statistical evidence of its efficacy, progress is slow. Prayer remains down the totem pole in western medicine, and still is not emphasized in the initial regiment of health therapy. Medical attitudes toward alternative therapies remain much more open in eastern medicine than in the west, as evidenced by centuries of acupuncture and alternative therapies such as reiki. Thankfully, this is changing, and Gary Schwarz has compiled excellent research on energy healing, vibrational medicine, and the effects of a conscious intention to heal (Schwartz & Simon, The Energy Healing Experiments: Science Reveals our Natural Power to Heal, 2007). We should expand the first line of defense to embrace the enormous potential of psychic and vibrational healing energies.

A poignant example of the reluctance to move quickly in traditional western medicine is reflected in the lack of serious attention our culture gives to the aforementioned medicineless hospitals in China. These medicineless hospitals usually get only patients that traditional medicine has given up on, yet their holistic and heart-based psychic methods have revealed some extraordinary cures. The New Mexican visionary scientist, Gregg Braden, has provided evidence of this particularly surprising cancer therapy to the western world in his writings and speeches. He has reported that small groups of healers began a meditation focused on healing cancerous tumors and capturing the energy of heart-based mental projection through direct focusing. The subsequent shrinking of cancerous tumors has repeatedly been captured on amazing video recordings. Gregg Braden has witnessed this personally, and when the videos of controlled spontaneous healings were shown to western cancer researchers, they accepted that the healings of seemingly hopeless cases were real and well documented. According to Braden, they were amazed, but rather than immediately perusing these successes in their own cancer research, they surprisingly said that we should research this in the western world "after we find a cure for cancer" (Braden, 2003). Startlingly, a predisposed perspective about what constitutes medical research did not allow these western researchers to believe that these medicineless healings might be instructive to their current search for a cancer cure.

Abraham Lincoln said that we are about as happy as we decide to be, adeptly capturing our ability to conquer the emotions of negative circumstances. In like manner, we are also about as healthy as we decide to be, as our mindset is instrumental in healing our bodies. Our physical bodies certainly have a constitution, so healings should employ all aspects of reality, but the power of the mind and spirit does us no good if downplayed rather than effectively researched and employed. Perhaps serious handicaps and structural maladies such as blindness and deafness are "charted" as part of a divine plan we are to experience, and some spirit guides tell us that these are agreed to before we incarnate into bodies. Esther and Jerry Hicks, drawing from *A Course of Miracles*, claim that every physical malady is somehow brought on by our own choices, whether consciously chosen or not (Hicks, 2006). These perspectives may seem fatalistic, but they indicate that, rather than being victims, we have a major part to play in our health throughout our time in the physical dimension. This includes having more innate healing ability than we generally give ourselves credit for having. By not sufficiently recognizing our innate healing abilities, we do not use them nearly as much as we could.

I am no expert in healing, but I have encountered or read about many cases of spirit-based healing. Most of them described the need to remain steadfast in believing that healing will occur. I noted that remaining unwavering without doubt in a spiritual healing adventure seems practically impossible to me, but those who put their attention on health and successfully refuse to entertain thoughts of sickness have overcome some serious maladies. For instance, the inspirational teacher, Wayne Dyer maintains that the leukemia labeled as medically incurable is no longer present in his body (Dyer, I Can Do It Conference, 2014).

You will not be surprised by now to discover that I decided to test this healing ability in my own life, which gives me a bit of personal testimony to add to the discussion of alternate spontaneous healings. I was inspired by a frequency-based technology called the AIM Program (aimprogram.com) (Lewis & Slawson, Sanctuary: The Path to Consciousness (Hay House, Inc.), 1998), also referred to as EMC[2]. Although it claims to be a spiritual technology that makes no claim to heal, many using AIM tell stories of overcoming illness through frequency-based spirituality.

## A Challenge in Personal Healing

Fifteen years ago I had root canal surgery on a tooth which my dentist said was so unusual that he did not want to tackle it. So he referred me to an orthodontist who said that the root structure of my tooth was unlike anything he had seen before. The tooth had three roots, which gave me fodder to joke that I was an alien rather than a human being. Regardless, I had an atypical root canal surgery. I had no symptoms of any problems after that until about eight years later, when I experienced obvious uncomfortable sensitivity in the gum at this root canal site. My regular dentist referred me to the same orthodontist who had done the original surgery. This specialist said that he was happy that his unusual surgery had served me well for many years, but there was a definite lack of bone in the area, so a second surgery would be required. He relayed that there was no hurry if I wanted to live with the uncomfortable situation, but the only solution for this structural problem would be another dental surgery. He essentially told me that this problem would not go away on its own.

Seeing an opportunity for self-healing, I decided not to believe this, and given that discomfort was a rather innocuous circumstance, embarked on a perfect chance to test self-healing. This dental ailment was bothersome but not immediately critical, which made it an almost perfect testing ground for applying some form of spiritual healing. Not relishing the expense and inconvenience of another dental surgery and intrigued by this new spiritual challenge, I decided to forego a second surgery and simply believe that the situation could be healed spiritually, regardless of what the orthodontist had said. My mindset was optimistically boosted by my participation in the AIM program. Doubt was not easy to avoid, particularly since I had heard Stephen Lewis, the founder of AIM, emphasize that structural anomalies like bones were particularly challenging to overcome with energetic healing (Lewis, Energetic Balancing via the AIM Program, 2004).

I set out quite imperfectly to heal this issue with an empowering belief in the God-given grace within me and the simple decision to heal. I would just "pray healing" and expect it to happen. Although I often encountered those pesky doubts, the discomfort was easing. The discomfort gradually subsided and only flared up occasionally, and I continued my regular dental visits for cleanings and checkups. A couple of years passed, and I changed dentists when my previous dentist quit accepting my provider's dental insurance. During a diagnosis at the new dentist's office, X-rays identified something slightly unusual at the site of this old root canal. Although my dentist said it probably was a minor concern, as I was no longer suffering discomfort, he suggested that I check out the peculiar situation with a specialist. In case my healing mission had partly failed, I decided to take this advice and set up an appointment with the recommended specialist, who was a different one than the surgeon for my initial root canal. This specialist's diagnostic series of x-rays and observations revealed a minor situation that seemed to be resolving on its own. She suggested that it should be left alone if it did not bother me.

Four years have passed, and again I changed dentists to one nearer my home. In conducting my regular dental care, my new dentist has never identified anything amiss at this site in my mouth. This may be an isolated example, and perhaps the first orthodontist's insistence that surgery was necessary may have been pecuniary. But I am perfectly happy to accept that the discomfort disappeared and this situation healed naturally and spiritually. Something that was supposed to require surgery gradually resolved itself through the power of prayer and intention. But this structural dental healing provided me with a snippet of personal evidence for the potential of spiritual-based healing.

A friend of mine, Jerry Joseph, relayed a more dramatic healing story that entailed assistance from his partner Ed who has passed on. Jerry was suffering from total renal failure that had reached the stage that he was expected to die at any time. He was alone at night, and told me the only thing visible was a small blue light on an IV machine in his room. Jerry heard his name called out in a voice he had not heard in years, from "the love of his life" who had passed away unexpectedly a few years earlier. Jerry was told not to be afraid. He then felt a hand placed on his chest. Instantly, "like turning on a switch", Jerry said his kidneys began to function (Baumeister, 2015). The unexpected and sudden return of normal function to a pair of kidneys that were in complete renal failure was verified by the medical equipment and staff monitoring his condition.

CHAPTER

# 22

# CONVERSATIONS
# ACROSS THE CHASM

OUR ACCULTURATED MINDS TEND TO get in the way when we attempt to heal
or get healing assistance from spiritual guides or loved ones who
have died. Just as we do not heal as well as we could if we tuned
into the magic of our own God-given healing abilities, we could
communicate better with departed loved ones if we removed the
barriers of disbelief about it.

The villain is doubt. One of the most frustrating facets of
attempting to communicate with someone who has died is that we
wonder whether we got a message or just an imagined coincidence.
Or worse, there is frustrating silence. We certainly are allowed hints,
or there would be no communication at all. There may be just
enough communication to indicate that it is real, but not enough
to convince us. If we are honest at the deepest level, our earthly
lives seem riddled with questions and doubt, and if we could only
communicate more clearly, we could remove the doubt.

Aye, there's the rub. In communicating with departed loves ones,
we once again find ourselves forced to live with evidence, when what
we want is proof. We want to get beyond believing something and

reach the blessed state of knowing it, which is a huge difference. So—no surprise—I asked my spirit guides the question, "Why this difficulty?" In fact, I have asked my spirit guides this question many times.

If this talk of spirit guides is hard to accept, particularly from someone who insists on wanting empirical evidence to believe anything, I felt the same doubts when I first started getting guidance messages in meditation. Although divine intervention is traditional Christianity, this spirit guide stuff is not, and I wondered whether these messages were authentic. Was this an intermediary communication with God? Or was it coming from a source that was sinister and ungodly? I am now comfortable with receiving spiritual wisdom in meditation, but I remain uncomfortable with sharing the term "spirit guide". Over time, I have realized that the messages always came from love, and by scriptural definition, God is love.

Getting back to the question, I have asked for spiritual guidance a number of times about why communication with departed spirits is not more obvious. If we could easily communicate with departed loved ones, it would give us solid circumstantial proof of consciousness survival after death. These guides are gentle with me, even though I am frustratingly persistent with this same question. I always get the same answer, which is that there is a spiritual value to not knowing, which I will expand on in a moment.

The pivotal point is that faith has its own inherent value, and sacred scriptures from various traditions express this, including the Christian gospel story of the apostle Thomas. Unlike the other apostles, Thomas had not yet witnessed the risen Christ, and he told the other apostles that he would not believe in their talk of Christ's resurrection until he had proof from his own senses, for which he has been dubbed "Doubting Thomas". When Thomas eventually encountered the resurrected Christ, Jesus told him that those who believe without having seen—that is, without the evidence of proof—are blessed.

So, it seems the creator of the universe does not want us to *know* all the answers while we are in our physical bodies and blesses that uncomfortable state of simply believing. As for our survival after death, if we had proof, we could cease the admonition to walk by faith and not by sight, toss faith aside, and walk by sight and not be faith.

So what would be wrong with that? Knowing seems far preferable to the cloud of unknowing that permeates our physical lives. Logically, however, not knowing is the only way our lives on earth really have value. If we knew—rather than believed—that our lives continue after we leave the body, there would be an insurmountable temptation to waste our physical incarnation on earth. We would fritter away the time until we got back to the real existence outside the body. Our lives would be analogous to a sports team knowing the final score of a game before the game is played, thereby reducing the motivation, interest, desire, and even much of the purpose for playing the game. If we knew that our earthly existence is just an uncomfortable way station, we may as well loll around in bed, waste time, and snuff out the body in order to leave this holding tank and get back to our real lives. This would defeat the purpose of incarnating in bodies, which is to learn from experiencing. Our physical perceptions buy into the mentality that "you only live once" since they are not convinced of an afterlife beyond the body. Because of this doubt about an afterlife, we are motivated to live our lives as fully as we can on earth, fulfilling our purpose for the earthly experience.

So the answer to my question of why communicating with the deceased is so difficult is that easy communication would effectively be proof of consciousness survival, and that proof would lead us to squander our physical incarnation. While not totally incommunicado with those who have departed, the element of doubt arising from incomplete communication with loved ones who have died motivates us to live. The few who really know that they are communicating with the "dead" have advanced to the point that they do not need doubt to make their earthly lives purposeful.

Another Christian scripture hints at this same lesson in a different way. In Chapter 16 of the Gospel of Luke, there is a story of the death of a rich man who had lived a less than exemplary life, ignoring the suffering needs of a poor beggar named Lazarus. Lazarus had spent his days at the rich man's gate, never receiving any help to alleviate his physical suffering. Lazarus dies first, and when the rich man dies, his spirit is in torment, so he begs Abraham to send someone from the dead to warn his brothers on earth to avoid a similar fate. His request is rebuffed, as he is told that his brothers must find their way without intervention. Again, this says that getting clear guidance from those who have passed on would seriously compromise the reason we are in bodies in the first place, which is to experience and learn and grow in a difficult environment that provides fertile opportunities for spiritual growth.

## ■ A Moving Message from my Dad

You may have guessed that I would not leave this topic without a personal story, and I consider my own experience a blessed and enlightening example of the use of electronics to cross the communication chasm. My dad passed away in 2004 just before the holiday celebrated in the United States as Flag Day. After my mother notified me of Dad's sudden passing, I was making the 130-mile drive from my home in Austin to my boyhood home just south of El Campo, Texas. In passing through the town of Bastrop, I noticed the highway was lined with American flags. Knowing that my Dad had served more than four years in World War II about a decade before I was born, I said out loud, "Look, Dad, they're flying flags everywhere for you." Immediately, the bell for my automobile seat belt began chiming repeatedly. This bell indicates that the seat belt is not fastened, but I was wearing my seat belt at the time. I could not turn off the chiming, so my thought shifted to a new frustrating obligation, to get this perplexing chiming repaired. After maybe twenty seconds it stopped chiming on its own, and thinking it might be a message, I said "Thank you, Dad". The seat belt bell never again chimed when my seat belt was buckled, until...

Several months later I was driving at highway speed on a farm-to-market road (FM 529) from my brother's house near Katy, Texas, back to Austin after attending a Rice University football game the night before. Again I was driving alone, and even though I was wearing my seat belt as usual, the chime indicating an unbuckled seat belt went off again. It had worked perfectly for several months with no recurring episodes of untimely chiming. I decelerated somewhat as I tugged on the seat belt, unclipping and clipping it to no avail, remembering that the only time this had happened was several months earlier on the day Dad died. Immediately, a car ran a stop sign and zipped across the road directly in front of my car. Had I not slowed in response to the seat belt chime, I could have collided with this other car at a deadly speed. Again I said, "Thank you, Dad." I never had that seat belt chime checked or repaired, and it never came on again once the seatbelt buckle was fastened.

That was about as clear a message from the spirit of my Dad that I could ever expect, yet there is always the thought that it could have been a coincidence of timing. I would have preferred hearing my Dad warn me in a recognizable voice. It is easy to believe that this was a message from my Dad, but I would prefer to *know* that it was a message from him. But, as my spirit guides tell me over and over, a bit of doubt is useful.

Speaking of doubt and its usefulness, on one late evening in July 2013, I was carrying on a conversation with my dear college friend, David Austin, sitting on a balcony that overlooked the beach at South Padre Island, Texas. The conversation moved to the question of whether our consciousness survives after death. You probably guessed that I am interested in this subject, so I wholeheartedly welcomed this shift in the conversation. The insights David shared with me had a tendency to be brilliant, and I very much wanted to get the perspective of one of the most intelligent people I knew. David had long ago rejected formalized religion, but he had a definite, albeit unusual, spiritual side. He would absorb himself in all sorts of literature on the topic. Despite my time in the Jesuits and my doctorate from the American Institute of Holistic Theology, he was far more literate about the Christian apologists than me. He often claimed to be an atheist, but it was quite apparent through years of honest communication that he was not, as he had a deep yearning for the divine and often shared spiritual revelations with me. Given our discussions, he was highly intrigued by the apparent existence of an observer and the observed residing simultaneously in the same mind, something I had experienced after a hemorrhage caused by a head injury I suffered in 1989.

Although David admitted to sharing a deep psychic bond with his mother while she was alive (although he would have resisted calling it by such hokey label), he had never received any messages from her after her death. The wine was kicking in by now, and I pointed out that maybe he was not listening well enough, and he huffed that the survival of consciousness after death was religious superstition. I countered that searching for the evidence of consciousness survival was not superstition, and he thanked me for reminding him of the distinction, saying that he had been prone to leap to that conclusion because it was late and he was tired. What I really want to share from this conversation is something I said before retiring for the night. I told him that if I died before him, I would deliver a clear message to him if I could. I requested that, if he predeceased me, that he do the same for me.

It was only about a month later, on August 15, 2013, that I received a telephone call from Ellen, David's dear friend and office manager. She cried as she relayed the tragic news that David had died unexpectedly that morning. A week later, I made the long drive from Austin to Pecos to attend and speak at David's memorial service. When I had asked that we share an afterlife message, I expected it would be many years before either of us passed on, but on that cross-Texas drive, I thought about my request to him from a month before.

A few months later, I did get a message from David. I was in a deep meditation when he told me that he had experienced the ultra-real phenomena we call a near-death experience, and that it was the same when actual death occurs. He said he had met up with his mother (who had passed on in the 1990s) and pointed out that, in another life, the two were soul mates. On earth, David would not have dared to speak of his mother as a soul mate. And I would not have dared to think it either, which is one piece of evidence that this message was not just imagination. This meeting was so overwhelming for him that he did not realize at the moment whether he was given the option to return to his earthly body. Neither would he have talked about an option to pass on (or not), but the message was quite clear and provided me some other information I did not know (which was very typical for David). He pointed out the difficulty of communicating from the other side, and for a person who possessed the technical wizardry he had on earth, this reaffirmed my belief that the chasm between those on the other side and those on the earth side is huge.

Although this message was real enough to be believable and had elements that showed it to be external to my mind, it was certainly not what I really wanted when I requested a message from David if he died before me. Of course, I was hoping for and envisioning a manifestation of a physical-looking form in my room, rather like a haunting. That may have made me yelp in fear, but without doubt, I would have preferred a haunting manifestation to the less intense message I received in a meditative state. Or I would have preferred

GARY G. PREUSS, PH.D.

hearing David's unmistakable corporeal voice. The message I got was real enough and peculiar enough to be David's, but the left-brained nerdy part of me obviously craved a message that placed it squarely in the realm of proof.

Once again, my spirit guides stepped in with the same message I had heard before and already shared with you. It sounded redundant to me, and it probably sounds redundant to you, but apparently we need repetition to believe it. A solid conviction that our physical lives are only temporary would destroy our motivation to experience and learn on earth. It makes logical sense, it is consistent with David's message that establishing communication from the beyond is difficult, and it explains why a chasm is placed between those living in the body and those who have left their bodies behind. If our discarnate loved ones communicated clearly with us on a regular basis, we would have little reason to incarnate on earth at all. We incarnate to learn and experience, and if we absolutely knew that we would continue in a more ideal home once our earthly time was over, we might ignore the present moment around us in favor of the destination. An economic analogy is deflation, which can cause economies to collapse because people do not buy goods and services if they believe that prices will keep falling. They delay their purchases until the price is more attractive. While on the road of life, our motivation to produce or experience would lack inspiration if we knew that we could accomplish our goals with far less effort after we die. Rather than waste our lives getting to a destination, we can experience the benefits of the road itself.

## ■ Suffering along the Road

During meditation, I also have asked about the age-old question of suffering—simply wanting to know why unpalatable events and emotions have to happen. Teilhard de Chardin, the Jesuit priest/ physicist/ author, was a visionary that struggled mightily with the seeming cruelty of a God who seemed distant to those desperately searching for union with the Creator. It is curious that Christ himself, in the Garden of Olives the night before he was crucified, asked if his impending cup of suffering had to be endured. It clearly did, but why?

Fulfilling our charted events is our part in being a co-creator. In attempting to explain suffering, Teilhard de Chardin speculated that God is not omnipotent, that he is struggling with creation. Stamping out suffering is part of that struggle and Teilhard argued that we were created to play a role in finding solutions. We then become co-creators. Teilhard never saw a contradiction between biological evolution and creationism during a time when fundamentalists insisted that only one of these possibilities could be true. All of creation, which is divine in its essence, continues to evolve in an ongoing way, and biological evolution is simply one of the ways it gets done. Our perceptions trick us into the illusion that God set the universe in motion and then abandoned it to function like clockwork without further intervention. Teilhard was convinced that the universe continues to be created as it evolves and that our own evolution is a piece of this ongoing creation. Charted events in our physical lives are how we do our part.

In my meditations, another answer I get repeatedly without regard for how many times I ask the same question is that we agree to undergo certain events in this life before we are even born. These events are "charted" as a type of contract for what we should learn while in our bodies. That is, our conscious minds come into an agreement with the divine that we will endure particular events during this lifetime. I am told that such charted events are determined and must be endured. A physicist might say that the wave function has already collapsed for a future event, meaning that whatever is charted is unalterable, but the particulars of that event may be. As an example of a charted event, assume that I have agreed to have an automobile accident during this incarnation, one where the brakes fail on my car. If it is charted that the brakes fail, it will happen in that way, and my spirit guides are not free to intervene. That is, they could not give me an intuitive warning to have my brakes fixed in advance. On the other hand, if I had only charted that I would have an automobile accident, with no particulars about what kind of accident, the particulars are alterable. My guides would then be free to give me intuitive hints to make such changes that will make the accident less onerous. Sylvia Browne spoke about receiving this same message from her spirit guides, noting that one could alter the particulars of many charted events. As I understand her perspective, if one has charted to have an automobile accident, the way we respond to our intuitive guidance can be the difference between a head-on fatal collision and a relatively innocuous fender-bender. Although charted events mean that the wave function has already collapsed in the future and is unalterable, the uncharted details are subject to change, and that is where our intuitive and psychic guidance can make a difference.

Although I sometimes do not like the answers, I have found that I am also guided as to exactly what can be altered and what cannot. All I need to do is prayerfully ask in meditation.

CHAPTER

# 23

# THIS JOURNEY HAS NO PERIOD

WE HAVE TAKEN QUITE A tour together. We have explored cosmological evidence for a purposeful creation of our universe, evidence for the reality of the "magic" of psi and the survival of consciousness, and communication with departed loved ones, all areas that experienced a blending of scientific and spiritual perspectives over the last few decades. The gap is narrowing, precisely because peculiar evidence is making science aware that the materialist paradigm has holes that only a more encompassing understanding can fill. The religious perspective also suffers from a tendency to hold inflexible beliefs, but scientific findings are reforming religious dogmas that do not fit the lived experiences of people.

Albert Einstein once bemoaned that "Science without religion is lame and religion without science is blind" (Einstein, 1941) Not surprisingly, it was Albert Einstein's thought experiments that were the impetus that eventually culminated in his relativity theories. It is fascinating that his insights were initially intuitive hunches, and these hunches exploded scientific thought into a new realm of reality. Science is now well on its way to acknowledging and accepting phenomena once deemed to be imagination and hallucination, while spirituality benefits from the verification of science. In a way, we find ourselves circling back to where we once were, to the combination of spirit and science initially embraced by Isaac Newton. Christian scriptures have long maintained that the kingdom is within us. It now seems that the eighteenth century's Immanuel Kant (1724-1804) was prescient when he speculated that it is in our "inner conscience" that we touch a reality more absolute than anything in science. Recent evidence confirms that he was on to something.

Striving to get beyond belief to a state of knowing is itself a major motivator that gives us a productive life. We experience, learn, and improve while in our physical bodies, so when we finally get to the other side of existence, we are a better creation than before we arrived on earth. As uncomfortable as it is not "to know" while we are in the body, the value of not knowing is indeed, as Christ said to Thomas, blessed.

Still, it is unfortunate that this book cannot close with a listing of firm conclusions. Conclusions regarding the paranormal remain slippery and subjective, and even what we perceive with our senses cannot be trusted. Our flawed perception can delude us both to accept paranormal phenomena that are not real and to reject paranormal phenomena that are.

Attempting to use the scientific paradigm to understand the paranormal is indeed woefully inadequate, but science is increasingly able to scratch the surface of reality, and those bits of progress reveal that much of what scientific materialism had rejected as unreal reflects reality better than materialist ideas. As science developed in its early days, it shied away from nonphysical concepts such as consciousness, but as it became more sophisticated, it is moving back toward them. After all, science now tells us that, with the huge gaps between anything particle-like, matter is 99.9999999 percent empty space anyway (Russell, 2002, p. 48). And because of the role that observation plays in the fuzzy quantum universe of waves and particles, the late German physicist Hans-Peter Dürr said simply that "matter is not made of matter" (Russell, 2002, p. 49) Now the evidence is on the side of a universe seemingly designed rather than random, since the probability that our universe formed randomly is infinitesimally small.

We have evidence that our brains do not perceive reality as it is but only the reality created as our minds process the sensory inputs to the brain, implying that matter is derived from the mind and not the mind from matter. It follows that the constraints of space and time "out there" are actually the constraints of our minds "in here", something Tibetan spirituality has maintained for ages. In Hinduism, Sir Nisargadatta Maharaj (a guru of Shiva Advaita spirituality) taught that the world is within you and not you in the world. This universal consciousness may be the meeting point between what has often been atheistic scientism and traditional religion. It includes universal communication via concepts such as nonlocality, allowing for phenomena such as telepathy, clairvoyance, precognition, and psychokinesis to exist. And because of the timeless nature of light, a light often observed in NDEs, this communication need not be affected by physical death, allowing for consciousness to remain in a timeless realm that always was and always will be. None of this can be said with certainly, but what appeared to be magic is now understood to be more than hopeful illusion. With evidence that spirituality is more than illusion, the power of prayer is enhanced, as we can increasingly walk by sight as well as faith alone.

It is time to end our journey, only to arrive at a level of unknowing. At least quantum physics has shown us that the materialist paradigm of reality, although useful for most of our physical activities, is incomplete and collapsing. We cannot truly understand physical reality because the process of observing it changes it. So the true nature of reality is something vastly different than it appears and far weirder and exciting than we can imagine. The fascinating payoff of closing the gap between science and spirituality is a realization that magic—or at least what we believed was magic—can be real.

# BIBLIOGRAPHY

*About Near-Death Experiences*. (2014, October 21). Retrieved from International Association for Near-Death Studies: http://iands. org/about-ndes.html

*Albert Einstein quotes*. (2015, April 28). Retrieved from Good Reads: http://www.goodreads.com/quotes/159397-everything-is-determined-the-beginning-as-well-as-the-end

Alexander, E. M. (2012). *Proof of Heaven: A Neurosurgeon's Journey into the Afterlife*. New York, NY: Simon & Schuster.

Alexander, E. M. (2013). Proof of Heaven. *Explore. Dream. Discover.* Indian Wells, California: Institute of Noetic Sciences 2013 Conference.

Arcangel, D. (2005). *Afterlife Encounters*. Charlottesville, Virginia: Hampton Roads.

Atwater, P. (2011). *Near-Death Experiences: The Rest of the Story* . Charlottesville, Virginia: Hampton Roads Publishing Company.

Atwater, P. (2014). *Dying to Know You: Proof of God in the Near Death Experience*. Faber, Virginia: Rainbow Ridge.

Bachrach, J. (2014). *Glimpsing Heaven: The Stories and Science of Life After Death*. Washington, D.C.: National Geographic Society.

Baumann, T. L. (2001). *God at the Speed of Light*. Virginia Beach, VA: ARE Press.

Baumeister, J. (2015, February 26). Telephone conversation. (G. Preuss, Interviewer)

Beischel, J. (2014). *From the Mouths of Mediums*. Tucson, Arizona: Windbridge Institute.

Betty, L. S. (2006). Are They Hallucinations or Are They Real? The Spirituality of Deathbed and Near-Death Visions. *Omega--Journal of Death and Dying, Volume 53 (1-2)*, 37-49.

Blanke, O., Landis, T., Spinelli, L., & Seeck, M. (2004). Out of Body Experience and Autoscopy of Neurological Origin. *Brain (127:2)*, 243-258.

Boltzmann, L. (n.d.). *The Second Law of Thermodynamics.*

Born, M. (1971). *The Born-Einstein Letters.* New York, NY: Walker and Company.

Braden, G. (Composer). (2003). Speaking the Lost Language of God: Awakening the Forgotten Wisdom of Prayer, Prophecy and the Dead Sea Scrolls. [N. C. Corporation, Performer] Niles, IL.

Braden, G. (Composer). (2003). Speaking the Lost Language of God: Awakening the Forgotten Wisdom of Prayer, Prophecy and the Dead Sea Scrolls. [N. Conant, Performer] Niles, Illinois.

Braden, G. (2008). "The Power and Promise of Spiritually Based Science. In *Measuring the Immeasurable).* Boulder, Colorado: Sounds True.

Braden, G. (Composer). (2010). Choice Point 2012: The Promise of our Future in the Cycles of the Past. [N. C. Corporation, Performer] Niles, IL.

Bruce, R. (2009). *Astral Dynamics: The Complete Book of Out-of-Body Experiences.* Charlottesville, Virginia: Hampton Roads Publishing.

Burnham, S. (2011). *The Art of Intuition.* New York, NY: Jeremy P. Tarcher/Penguin.

*California Institute of Integral Studies.* (2011, June). Retrieved from Online Academic Catalog: www.ciis.edu

Callahan, G. (2005, June 9). Scientism Standing in the Way of Science: An Historical Precedent to Austrian Economics. *Mises Daily,* pp. 1-5.

Carroll, R. T. (2011, May 3). *Psi assumption* . Retrieved from The Skeptics Dictionary 2005: http://www.skepdic.com/psiassumption.html

Carter, C. (2010). *Science and the Near-Death Experience: How Consciousness Survives Death.* Rochester, Vermont: Inner Traditions.

Carter, C. (2012). *Science and the Afterlife Experience.* Rochester, Vermont: Inner Traditions.

Caudill, M. (2012). *Impossible Realities.* Charlottesville, Virginia: Hampton Road Publishing.

*Center for Consciousness Studies.* (2014). Retrieved from University of Arizona: www.consciousness.arizona.edu

Choquette, S. (Composer). (1993). Your Psychic Pathway: Listening to the Guiding Wisdom of your Soul. [N. C. Corporation, Performer] Wheeling, Illinois.

Cicoria, T., & Cicoria, J. (2014, Fall). Vital Signs. *International Association for Near-Death Studies, Volume 33, No. 3,* p. 4.

Davies, P. (1983). *God & The New Physics.* New York, NY: Simon & Schuster .

Dillard, S. (2013). *You are a Medium.* Woodbury, Minnesota: Llewellyn Publications.

Dosa, D. (2011). *Making Rounds with Oscar: The Extraordinary Gift of an Ordinary Cat.* New York, NY: Hachette Books.

Dow, C. (2010). Writing Reality: Paranormal Experiences in Jeffrey J. Kripal's Authors of the Impossible. *Rice University Magazine,* pp. 19-21.

Druckman, D. a. (1988). *Enhancing Human Performance:Issues, Theories and Techniques .* Washington, D.C.: National Academy Press.

Du Tertre, N. (2012). *Psychic Intuition.* Pompton Plains, NJ: 2012.

Dupre, J. (2001). *Human Nature and the Limits of Science.* Oxford, England: Clarendon Press.

Dyer, D. W. (Composer). (2012). Secrets of Manifesting: A Spiritual Guide for Getting What You Want. [I. Hay House, Performer] Carlsbad, California.

Dyer, W. (1989). *You'll See It When You Believe It*. New York, NY: W. Morrow.

Dyer, W. (2014). I Can Do It Conference. Austin, Texas: Hay House, Inc.

Einstein, A. (1941). Symposium on Science, Philosophy and Religion. New York, NY.

Faggin, F. (2015). The Nature of Consciousness. *The 16th International Conference of the Institute of Noetic Sciences*. Oak Brook, Illinois: The Institute of Noetic Sciences.

Filippenko, A. P. (Composer). (2007). Understanding the Universe: An Introduction to Astronomy, 2nd Ed., Lecture 3:28. [T. T. Company, Performer] Chantilly, Virginia.

Foundation, W. (2011, May 24). *Miracle of the Sun*. Retrieved from Wikipedia: http://en.wikipedia.org/wiki/Miracle_of_the_Sun

Frost, R. (1920). *The Poetry of Robert Frost, Mountain Interval*. . New York, NY: Henry Holt and Company .

Gerald L. Schroeder, P. (1997). *The Science of God: The Convergence of Scientific and Biblical Wisdom*. New York, NY: Free Press.

Goethe, J. W. (1749-1832). *Brainy Quote*. Retrieved from http://www.brainyquote.com/quotes/quotes/j/johannwolf107491.html

Green, C. a. (1975). *Apparitions*. London: Hamish Hamilton, Ltd.

Greyson, B. (2014, October 5). Does Consciousness need a Brain? - Evidence for Reincarnation. *https://www.youtube.com/watch?v=yosn_GHYiR4*. Dehradun, India: Karma Rinchen Dawa, www.YouTube.com.

Gribbin, J. (May 1, 1996). *Schrodinger's Kittens and the Search for Reality: Solving the Quantum Mysteries*. New York, New York: Back Bay Books.

Harraldson, E. (1994). Spontaneous Cases: Apparitions of the Dead. In e. Emily Cook and Deborah Delanoy, *Research in Parapsychology*. London: The Scarecrow Press.

Hart, H. e. (1956). Six Theories about Apparitions . *Proceedings from the Society for Psychical Research, part 185*, (pp. 203-204).

Hawking, S. (1988). *A Brief History of Time*. New York, NY: Random House Publishing. Retrieved from A Brief History of Time: http://hyperphysics.phy-astr.gsu.edu/nave-html/faithpathh/hawking.html

Hawkins, D. (1995). *Power vs Force: The Hidden Determinants of Human Behavior*. Sedona, Arizona: Veritas Publishing (5th printing).

Hawkins, D. R. (2005). *Truth vs. Falsehood: How to Tell the Difference*. Toronto, Ontario, Canada: Axial Publishing.

Herbert, N. (1985). *Quantum Reality: Beyond the New Physics*. New York, NY: Anchor Books.

Hicks, E. a. (2006). *The Amazing Power of Deliberate Intent: Living the Art of Allowing*. Carlsbad, California: Hay House, Inc.

Hines, T. (2003). *Pseudoscience and the Paranormal* . Buffalo, New York: Prometheus Books.

Hodgson, R. (2011, April 27). *Australian Dictionary of Biography: Online Edition*. Retrieved from Richard Hodgson (1855-1905): http://www.adb.online.anu.edu.au/biogs/A040457b.htm

Holden, J. M. (2014, May 27). *Consciousness/Life After Death?* Center for Spiritual Living, Austin, Texas.

Holland, J. (2002). "I Can Do it". Atlanta, GA: Hay House.

Holland, J. (2008). (". C. Conference, Performer) Las Vegas, Nevada.

Horgan, J. (November 25, 1996). Life, Life Everywhere. *Scientific American*.

Howard, E. D.-R. (2005, October). Finding and Correcting Flawed Research Literatures. *The Humanist Psychologist*, pp. 33 (4): 293-303.

Hoyle, F. (November, 1981). The Universe: Past and Present Reflections. *Engineering and Science*, 8-12.

Irwin, H. J. (1989). *An Introduction to Parapsychology*. Jefferson, North Carolina: McFarland Press.

Irwin, H. J. (1989). *An Introduction to Parapsychology*. Jefferson, North Carolina:: McFarland Press.

Janssen, S. (2014, Fall). Whispering in the Shadows: A Hospice Social Worker Learns to Ask About NDEs. *Vital Signs*, pp. 11-13.

Jauregui, A. P. (2007). *Epiphanies: Where Science and Miracles Meet.* New York, NY: Atria Books.

Jeans, J. (1931). *The Mysterious Universe.* Whitfish, Montana: Kessinger Publishing (reprint).

Lewis, S. (2004, April 20). Energetic Balancing via the AIM Program. *Free Lecture and Demonstration with Stephen Lewis.* Escondido, California: EMC-2.

Lewis, S., & Slawson, E. (1998). *Sanctuary: The Path to Consciousness (Hay House, Inc.).* Retrieved from The AIM Program of Energetic Balancing: aimprogram.com

MacDougall, D. (2010, January 27). *The 21 Grams Theory.* Retrieved from Historic Mysteries: http://www.historicmysteries.com/the-21-gram-soul-theory/

Markwick, B. (1978). The Soal-Goldney Experiments with Basil Shackleton: New Evidence of Data Manipulation. *The Journal for the American Society of Psychical Research, Volume 56*, 250-277. Retrieved from Markwick, B. "The Soal-Goldney Experiments with Basil Shackleton: New Evidence of Data Manipulation." The Journal for the American Society of Psychical Research. 56 (1978

McTaggart, L. (2003). *The Field.* New York, NY: Harper Collins.

Mikkelson, B. (2013, December 28). *Choir Non-Quorum.* Retrieved from Snopes.com: http://www.snopes.com/luck/choir.asp

*Miracle of the Sun.* (2015, April 22). Retrieved from Wikipedia: http://en.wikipedia.org/wiki/Miracle_of_the_Sun

Moody, R. (2001). *Life After Life (3rd edition).* New York: Harper Collins Publishers.

Myers, F., & Stevenson, I. (1982). The Contribution of Apparitions to the Evidence for Survival. *Journal of the Society of Psychical Research, 76*, 349.

Odling-Smee, L. (2007, June 29). The Lab that asked the Wrong Questions. *Nature (446)*, 10-11. Retrieved from http://intl.emboj. org/nature/journal/v446/n7131/full/446010a.html

*Olivier Costa de Beauregard (1911-2007).* (n.d.). Retrieved from http:// www.costa-de-beauregard.com/fr/

Oschner, J. (1974). The Silva Method. Houston, Texas: www. silvamethod.com.

Penrose, R. (1979). Singularities and time-asymmetry. In R. Penrose, & S. W. Israel (Ed.), *General Relativity: An Einstein Centenary Survey* (p. 179). Cambridge, England: Cambridge University Press.

Preuss, E. E. (1989). *Conversational interview.* El Campo, Texas.

Raaberg, M. (1976). Sociology Conversation. *University of Chicago.* Chicago, Illinois: University of Chicago.

Raatz, J. (2013). *Can Science Find the Soul?* Retrieved from YouTube. com: https://www.youtube.com/watch?v=Q6ZY9Lgbb8Y

Radin, D. (1997). *The Conscious Universe: The Scientific Truth of Psychic Phenomena.* New York, NY: Harper Collins.

Radin, D. (2006). *Entangled Minds.* New York: Paraview Publications.

Radin, D. (2013). *15th International Conference of the Institute of Noetic Sciences.* Indian Wells, California: Institute of Noetic Sciences.

Radin, D. (2013). *Supernormal.* Petaluma, California: The Institute of Noetic Sciences.

Radin, D. P. (2013). Mind and Light. *Institute of Noetic Sciences.* Indian Wells, California.

Randhawa, J. (2006). *What is Metaphysics? Where Physics and Metaphysics Merge.* Retrieved from http://www.whatismetaphysics. com/metaphysical-ezine-4.html

Reissig, M. (2015, January 14). *Passive Aggressive Behavior.* Retrieved from MyPulseNews: http://mypulsenews.com/passive-aggressive-behavior/

Ring, K. a. (1999). *Near Death and Out of Body Experiences in the Blind.* Palo Alto, California: William James Center for Consciousness Studies.

Ring, K., & Lawrence, M. (Summer, 1993). Further Evidence for Veridical Perception During Near-Death Experiences. *Journal of Near-Death Studies.*

Roth, R. (Composer). (1999). Divine Dialogue. [N. C. Corporation, Performer] Niles, Illinois.

Rubin, B. J. (Writer), & Zucker, J. (Director). (1990). *Ghost* [Motion Picture]. USA.

Russell, P. (2002). *From Science to God: A Physicist's Journey into the Mystery of Consciousness.* Novato, CA: New World Library.

Sabom, M. (1998). *Light and Death.* Grand Rapids, Michigan: Zondervan Publishing.

Schmeidler, G. (1973). *Who is Gertrude Schmeidler?* Retrieved from Parapsychological Association: http://archived.parapsych.org/members/g_schmeidler.html

Schwartz, G. (2002). *The Afterlife Experiments: Breakthrough Scientific Evidence of Life After Death.* New York NY: Pocket Books.

Schwartz, G. E. (2011). *The Sacred Promise: How Science is Discovering Spirit's Collaboration with Us in Our Daily Lives .* New York, NY: Atria Books.

Schwartz, G. E., & Simon, W. L. (2007). *The Energy Healing Experiments: Science Reveals our Natural Power to Heal.* New York, NY: Atria Books.

*Semmelweis, Ignaz (1818-1865).* (2013). Retrieved from Science Museum Brought to Life: http://www.sciencemuseum.org.uk/broughttolife/people/ignazsemmelweis.aspx

Sheldrake, R. (2011). *Dogs That Know When Their Owners Are Coming Home: And Other Unexplained Powers of Animals.* New York: Broadway Books (revised).

Smolinski, J. (2010, June 10). *Psychic Sylvia Browne on Ghosts, Angels, Men, and Her New Book 10 June 2010. 28 May 2011 .* Retrieved from Lemondrop.com: http://www.lemondrop.com/2010/06/10/psychic-sylvia-browne-on-ghosts-angels-men-and-her-new-book/6

Snobelen, S. (2011, March 14). *Religious Views of Isaac Newton.* Retrieved from http://en.wikipedia.org/wiki/Isaac_Newton's_religious_views

Stefko, J. (2009). *What Was Walter J. Levy's Parapsychology Scandal?. 2009. 19 May 2011.* Retrieved from .http://www.suite101.com/content/parapsychology-walter-j-levy-jr-scandal-a120060Supersense book

Studies, C. f. (2011, January 6). *Toward a Science of Consciousness.* Retrieved from Center for Consciousness Studies, University of Arizona : http://consciousness.arizona.edu

Swimme, B. (1990). *Canticle of the Cosmos.* Boulder, Colorado: Sounds True Audio Courses.

Tart, C. T. (2009). *The End of Materialism: How Evidence of the Paranormal is Bringing Science and Spirit Together.* Oakland, California: New Harbinger Publications.

Thayer, H. e. (1953). Newton's Philosophy of Nature: Selections from his Writings. In I. Newton, *Principia Book III.* New York: Hafner Library of Classics.

*The Silva Method.* (2011, June 2). Retrieved from 2 June 2011. <http://www.silvamethod.com>

Tompkins, P. a. (2002). *The Secret Life of Plants.* New York, NY: Harper Perennial.

Topa, W. (. (2011). *The Missing Link: Neuroscience and Indigenous Wisdom.* Petaluma, California: The Institute of Noetic Sciences: The Noetic Post.

Tucker, J. B., & Stevenson, I. (2008). *Life Before Life: Children's Memories of Previous Lives.* New York, NY: St. Martin's Griffin.

Viereck, G. S. (1929, October 26). What Life Means to Einstein. *The Saturday Evening Post,* pp. 17, 110-117.

Vlastimil Hart, P. N. (2013). *Dogs are sensitive to small variations of the Earth's Magnetic Field.* Retrieved from Frontiers in Zoology: http://www.frontiersinzoology.com/content/pdf/1742-9994-10-80.pdf

Westfall, R. S. (1977). *The Construction of Modern Science: Mechanisms and Mechanics*. New York and Melbourne: Cambridge University Press.

Wigner, E. (1983). Remarks on the Mind-Body Problem. In J. A. Wheeler, *Quantum Theory and Measurement*. Elizabeth, New Jersey: Princeton University Press.

Wise, R. (Director). (1965). *The Sound of Music* [Motion Picture].

# INDEX

## Symbols

9-11  13, 155

## A

accreditation  23
*A Course of Miracles*  175
aether
  ether  15–16, 81
  afterlife  92, 98–101, 103,
    119–120, 130, 138, 144,
    148, 185
AIM Program
  Energetic Matrix Church of
    Consciousness  176, 197
aircraft crashes  54
Alexander, Eben  107, 121–122
alpha state  viii
Alvarado Zingrone Institute for
  Research and Education  41
Ambady, Nalini  50
American Institute of Holistic
  Theology
  AIHT  156–157, 184
  American Society for Psychical
    Research  34
Anasazi  152–153
*anatta*  100
animal intuition  71
anthropic principle  4

Arcangel, Dianne  138
Aristotle  29, 67
Arizona  85, 136, 153, 192, 196
Arizona, University of  24, 40, 135,
    194, 200
Arthur Findlay College  132
atomic forces  1–2, 4, 32, 42
Atwater, P.M.H.  43

## B

Bachrach, Judy  117
Baumann, T. Lee  xiii, 192
Bayless, Raymond  130
Beischel, Judy  126
Bell's Theorem  77
Betty, L. Stafford  121–122
*Bhagavad Gita*  xii
Bharucha, Jamshed  50
Big Bang  7–8, 10, 17, 105, 129
black holes  78
Blanke, Olaf  121
Blavatsky, Madame  34
blind sightedness  68
Bohr, Neils  14, 76
Boltzmann, Ludwig  6, 193
Boundary Institute  13
brain  viii, xvii, 14, 46, 50, 68–69,
    79, 82, 91–93, 95–96, 99,

101, 104–111, 113, 115–116,
121, 191
Brenner, Wendy 130
Broglie, Louis de 48
Browne, Sylvia 62–63, 129,
188, 199
Bruce, Robert 111
Buddhism 100

## C

California Institute of Integral
Studies 24, 40, 193
California State University at
Bakersfield 121
*Canticle of the Cosmos* 2, 200
carbon 8–9, 49
Carter, Brandon 9
Carter, Chris 98, 140, 142, 144
Caudill, Maureen 36, 194
Center for Consciousness Studies
24, 40, 194, 198, 200
Center for the Study of Anomalous
Psychological Processes 41
Chicago, University of xvi, 198
Chi-lel Qigong 27
Choquette, Sonia 28, 88, 162, 194
Christianity xii, 101, 108, 180
Cicoria, Tony 115
Clark, Kimberley 116
clothing 122, 141, 143, 145, 152
coincidence ix, 55, 57, 72, 116, 123,
148, 158, 179, 183
Committee for Skeptical
Inquiry 36
consciousness x–xiii, 4, 13–14, 16,
24–25, 40, 43–44, 46, 48, 51,

56, 69–70, 73, 76, 78–79, 81–
82, 85–86, 89–103, 105–108,
110–117, 121–125, 128–129,
133–135, 142, 144, 148, 150,
154, 180–181, 184, 189–191,
194, 200
Cooper, Callum E. 130
Cooper, Sharon 118
Copenhagen interpretation 48
Copernicus 31
cosmology x, xiii, xvii, xxi, 30, 81
Costa de Beauregard, Olivier
80, 198
crystals 37
Curie, Marie 16

## D

Dad 182–183
David Austin 127
Davies, Paul 9–10, 194
death wish 56
De Chardin, Teilhard 80, 187
Descartes 33
De Sitter, Willem 2
dogmatism 21
Doubting Thomas 96, 180
dreams 55, 111, 163
Duke University xxi, 40
Dupre, John 33, 194
Dürr, Hans-Peter 190
Du Tertre, Nancy 68
Dyer, Wayne 3, 166, 170, 175,
194–195
Dyson 69
Dyson, G.M. 69

## E

Edward, John 35
Einstein, Albert 2, 11–14, 16,
    47–48, 65, 76–77, 129, 189,
    192–193, 195, 198, 200
El Campo xix, 182, 198
    Texas 143
electromagnetic energy xiii, 13,
    24, 42, 45, 70, 74, 92, 105
electroreception 68
energy field theory 86
energy healing 173
entanglement 12, 14–15, 44, 77
entropy 4–6, 10
ESP 23, 37, 40, 67
expansion 2, 4, 10

## F

Faggin, Federico 14, 195
faith xv, xvi, 3, 34, 79, 85, 89–90,
    92–93, 101, 103, 122, 148,
    160–161, 180–181, 191
Feynman, Richard xii
Francis of Assisi 102, 169
fraud 32–35, 61, 136, 141

## G

Galileo 31
Global Consciousness Project 45
God xii, xv, 9, 13, 25, 28–30, 32,
    77, 80, 95, 103, 114, 120,
    146, 151, 161, 168–169,
    171–172, 177, 179–180, 187,
    192–195, 199
God and the New Physics 9

Gospel xii, 124, 169, 173, 182
gravitational force 9
gravity 1, 3–4, 30, 32, 42, 78
Green, Celia and McCreery,
    Charles 140
Greyson, Bruce 41, 99
Grout, Pam 139
guidance x, xviii, 127, 139, 155–
    158, 160, 164, 170, 172, 182

## H

Hancock, Graham 106
Haraldsson, Erlendur 140
Harmon, Joyce 117
Hart, Hornell 141
Hawking, Stephen 10, 196
Hawkins, David xiii, 25–26, 44,
    161–162, 196
healing xiv, xix, 25, 27, 64, 67, 77,
    92, 156, 160, 173–179
HeartMath Institute 13
Heisenberg 14
Henry, Richard Cohn 78
Herbert, Nick 48, 80
Hicks, Esther and Jerry 175
hidden variables theory 48
Hodgson, Richard 34, 196
Holden, Janice Miner 113, 120, 122
Holland, John 84–86, 88–89, 133,
    135, 137, 148, 162, 196
Horgan, John 3, 196
Hoyle, Sir Fred 5, 8–9, 196
Hubble, Edwin 2
Humason, Milton 2
Hyman, Ray 36

## I

infinity 4, 79, 108
Institute of Noetic Sciences
    IONS xxi, 23–24, 41, 54,
    59, 64–65, 192, 195,
    198, 200
Institute of Parapsychology
    34, 40
International Association of Near
    Death Studies
    IANDS 113
Irwin, Harvey 61, 196

## J

Jahn, Robert 40
James Chaffin case 144
Jauregui, Ann 20, 197
Jeans, Sir James 78, 197
Jerry Joseph 178
Jesuits xvi, 94, 120, 184
John of God 168
Journal of Parapsychology 40
Judaism 100

## K

Kant, Immanuel 190
Kepler, Johannes 31
kinesiology 25
Koestler Parapsychology Unit 41
Koran xii
Kripal, Jeffrey 43

## L

Lazarus 182
Levy, Walter J. 34, 200

Lewis, Stephen 177, 197
light xii, xvii, 2, 12, 15–17, 36, 45,
    47, 54, 59, 62, 68–69, 76–78,
    81, 113, 115–116, 120, 128–
    129, 140, 178, 191
light wave xii, 12, 59, 64–65, 76,
    79, 187–188
Lincoln, Abraham 175
Lister, Joseph 21
Liverpool Hope University 41
lottery 3, 58–63, 172
Lowery, Pam Reynolds 117
Lubbock xix

## M

MacDougall, Duncan 94
magnetic fields 13, 73
magnetism 32–33
magneto reception 73
many universes theory 48
materialism xii, 21, 31, 38, 42, 75,
    79–81, 190
materialistic determinism 21
McTaggart, Lynne 25, 40, 60, 65,
    70, 197
medicineless hospitals 27, 174
meditation 59, 66, 88–89, 150,
    152, 156–157, 160, 163, 174,
    185–186, 188
mediumship 25, 35, 69, 84–88,
    127, 132, 135–136, 139
Merle 143
meta-analysis xi, 59, 62, 64
Michelson-Morley experiment 12
Miracle of the Sun 145, 195, 197
miracles xix, 25, 167–171, 173

Mishra, Swarnlata 98
Moody, Raymond xx, 38, 113, 120,
    154, 197
morphogenesis 28
multicellular organisms 6
multiple personality disorder 93
Myers, Fred 141

# N

National Academy of Sciences
    23, 39
National Science Foundation 38
near-death experiences
    NDE xii, xx, 14, 25, 38, 43, 47,
        100, 103, 107–108, 113–
        115, 118, 121–123, 128,
        148, 154, 185
    Nebraska 28, 53, 155
Neurocomputation 47
Newton, Isaac 29–32, 48, 81,
    190, 200
Niagara Falls 137
nonlocality 12, 14, 47, 76, 191

# O

Occam's razor 5, 11, 135
occult 30, 32–34
odds ix, xix, 3, 11–12, 46, 54, 60–
    61, 64–65
Olam Ha Ba 100
Orloff, Judith 162
other side ix, xi, 2, 119, 128, 131,
    139, 145–146, 185, 190
out-of-body experiences 25, 69,
    96, 107, 110–111, 115
Owen Howerson case 142

# P

Palladino, Eusapia 34
Palmer, John 140
Palmquist, Stephen R. 78
paradigm ix, xi, 20–22, 28, 31, 41–
    42, 47–48, 50, 55, 75, 80–81,
    104–105, 107, 113, 189–191
paranormal x–xi, xiv–xv, xvii–xx,
    12–14, 22–26, 29, 34–35,
    37–45, 47, 49–50, 52, 62, 65,
    70, 73, 75, 121, 130, 151, 161,
    163, 190
parapsychic science x
Parapsychological Association
    45, 199
parapsychology 35–36, 61, 71, 200
Parapsychology Foundation 41
Pasteur, Louis 21
PEAR xxi, 40
Penrose, Roger 10
perceptions xi, xvii, 16–17, 38, 45,
    76–77, 91, 95, 102, 112, 115,
    118, 138, 181, 187
Peter the Apostle 170
philosophy xvi, 4, 29, 31–33,
    77, 168
photoelectric effect 47
Planck, Max 47
Plato 29, 78
positivism xvi
Powerball 54, 60
prayer xiii, 25, 27, 44, 53, 64, 66,
    77, 88, 147, 150, 152, 157,
    164, 169–170, 173, 178, 191

precognition  28, 40, 55, 67, 134, 191
Price, Harry  34
Princeton University  xxi, 13, 40, 45–46, 64, 201
probability  xxi, 1, 3–5, 9–10, 54, 60, 100, 191
Project Alpha  35
proof  xv, 2, 4, 16, 18, 39, 42, 53, 82, 93, 142, 168, 179–181, 186
*Proof of Heaven*  107, 121, 192
psi  x–xi, xiv, xviii, 20–25, 31, 34–37, 39–42, 44–45, 47, 51–53, 57, 59, 61, 63–69, 71–72, 74, 77–78, 80–81, 85, 88–89, 92, 111–113, 132, 135, 139, 150–151, 154, 156, 166, 172, 189
psychic abilities  vii, x, 25, 33, 35, 38, 44, 51, 59, 62, 66, 171

## Q

quantum physics  xi–xiii, 12, 14, 18, 30, 44, 47–48, 57, 64–65, 75–76, 78–80, 191

## R

Raatz, Johanan  80
Radin, Dean  41, 54–55, 57, 59–60, 65, 198
Ramos, Carlos  130
Randi, James  35
realism  76
reality  ix, xii–xiv, xvii–xviii, 6, 13–15, 17, 21, 27, 39, 42, 44–45, 47–48, 50, 52, 62–64, 66, 70, 72, 75–76, 78–81, 88, 107,

111, 113–114, 118, 132, 136, 150, 152, 154, 175, 189–191
religion  xiii, 21, 25, 33, 80, 92, 136, 138, 184, 189, 191
remote viewing  36, 40
resurrection  92, 101–102
retroactive prayer  65
Rhine Research Center  40
Rice University  ix–xi, 43, 164–165, 183, 194
Ring, Kenneth  112–113, 118, 198–199
Rogo, D. Scott  130
Roll, W.G.  45
Roth, Ron  199
Russell, Bertrand  32
Russell Grant College of Psychic Studies  41
Russell, Peter  79

## S

Sabom, Michael  115–116
Sagan, Carl  154
Sai Baba, Sathya  168–169
Schmeidler  199
Schmeidler, Gertrude  56, 199
Schopenhauer, Arthur  97
Schrodinger's cat  13
Schroeder, Gerald  6, 195
Schwarz, Gary  35–36, 174
scientism  17, 21, 38, 51, 75, 92, 101, 191
scopaesthesia  28
second law of thermodynamics  4
Semmelweis, Ignaz  21–22, 199

senses xvii, 1, 16, 67–69, 71, 73, 78,
    95, 110–112, 121, 146, 148,
    180, 190
Sheldrake, Rupert 28, 71
Sidgwick, Henry 41
Silva, Jose 62, 172
Silva Mind Control vii–ix, 38, 62,
    88, 151, 198, 200
Singularities and time-
    asymmetry 10
*Skeptical Inquirer* 35–36
Slipher,Vesto 2
Smith, Gordon 85
Soal-Goldney experiments 34
Society for Psychical Research 41,
    135, 195
special relativity xvii, 16, 77
spirit-based healing 175
Spiritual Exercises
    of Saint Ignatius Loyola 88
spirituality x–xiii, 12, 24, 33, 44, 51,
    136, 176, 184, 189, 191
Stanford Research Institute 40
statistical significance viii, xiv, 22,
    24, 53, 61, 65
statistics ix, xiv, xvi, 3, 12, 46, 59,
    113, 119
Stevenson, Ian 41, 99, 154
supernatural 14, 29, 31–32, 74
superstition xi, xvii, 8, 18, 20–21,
    32, 184
Swimme, Brian 2, 200

**T**

Targ, Elisabeth 25
Tart, Charles T. 21

telepathy 28, 40, 77, 126, 191
telephone 97, 130, 184
Tiller, William 14
time xvii
Topa, Wahinkpe 50
Transpersonal Psychology
    Research Unit 41
tsunami 55
Tucker, Jim 154
Tufts University 50
Twin Towers 55

**U**

unicellular organisms 6
universal consciousness 82
universe ix–xi, xiii, xv, xxi, 1–6,
    8–12, 14–15, 17, 30, 45,
    47–48, 70, 76, 78–79, 92, 94,
    105–106, 108, 111, 123, 128,
    150, 173, 181, 187, 189–190
University of Edinburgh 41
University of Virginia 40, 99,
    114, 154

**V**

Venus 49
veridical perceptions 115
vibrational medicine 173–174
Von Goethe, Wolfgang 152
Von Neumann, John 79

**W**

Wasserman, G.D. 45
West Side Church 53
    Beatrice, Nebraska 53
Wheeler, John 1, 201

Wigner, Eugene  79
Winchester mountain range  153
Windbridge Institute  xxi, 85, 136,
     138, 147, 192

## Y

Yuri  115

## Z

Zero Point Field  70

Printed in the United States
By Bookmasters